TIGER MOTH

New, pristine, unruffled: a production Tiger Moth anticipates her wings in the final assembly shop at Hatfield. Who would have prophesied that half a century later the Type would have joined the immortals?

TIGER MOTH

A TRIBUTE

STUART McKAY

ORION
BOOKS
NEW YORK

To the memory of Alan S. Butler,
without whose generous enthusiasm
no de Havilland Moth might have
aired her delicate wings.

First published in 1987 by Airlife Publishing Ltd.

Published in the United States in 1988 by Orion Books, a division of Crown
Publishers, Inc., 225 Park Avenue South, New York, N.Y. 10003. ORION is
a trademark of Crown Publishers.

Library of Congress details available.

ISBN: 0-517-56864-0

Printed in England, by Livesey Ltd., Shrewsbury.

Contents

Preface

Since the October day in 1931 when Hubert Broad, chief test pilot to the de Havilland Aircraft Company, first flew the DH Type 82 from the muddy acres of Stag Lane aerodrome, the Tiger Moth has been recognised worldwide as the definitive biplane trainer.

During its formative years, the UK Tiger Moth was built in small numbers for the Royal Air Force, whilst de Havilland's sales organisation worked hard to establish the DH82 as standard training equipment overseas. Small scale production was licensed in Norway and Sweden for local consumption.

Club or privately owned Tiger Moths were rare beasts before 1937, and most of the few civil registered machines owed much to the roving air circuses where they were extensively used for stunting. The publicity and operational experience gained was invaluable to the makers.

The civilian administered RAF Reserve Schools in Great Britain were allocated Tiger Moths built to the upgraded "A" specification beginning in March 1933. (Licence built DH82As also were manufactured in Norway, Sweden and Portugal.) Each school machine carried civil registration letters and an easily distinguishable and distinctive colour scheme. Upon the outbreak of war, the reds, yellows, blues and mauves disappeared under a unified camouflage paint scheme, although civil identities were incongruously displayed on fuselage sides for some months.

Three DH82As were built by students of the DH Technical School at Hatfield and operated by the London Aeroplane Club. One was sold in France in 1937, but the remaining two were enrolled into the war effort and gave their all in 1940 and 1941.

The Commonwealth Air Training Plan utilised thousands of Tiger Moths built in Great Britain, Australia, New Zealand and Canada. At the beginning of hostilities, almost the entire inventory of the Bristol Reserve School was bodily shifted from Gloucestershire and Wiltshire to India, where the aircraft were civilian registered to become an instant training unit on behalf of the Indian Government.

Thousands of Allied airmen learned their craft on the Tiger Moth operating from the sun-drenched plains of India and Africa to the frozen prairies of Central Canada; from the Elementary Flying Training Schools in the Antipodes to the Grading Schools of Great Britain, where many an aspirant flew his miserly allocation of hours through seasonal mists and industrial haze, whilst infinitely tolerant instructors attempted to assess individual abilities with as much sympathy as they were permitted under the prevailing system.

Mass production of the Tiger Moth finished in 1944, the last aeroplanes flying away from their UK motor factory straight into storage pending a decision on their fate. Eventually, many found their way overseas to assist in the re-establishment of military and civil flying schools where subsequently they were joined by large numbers of reconditioned aircraft, released from RAF service as the vast training machine wound rapidly down.

Co-ownership groups and formal flying clubs were constituted using surplus Tiger Moths sold and bought for between £50 and £150; many in fly-away condition. New engines were offered by the auctioneers in original maker's crates for an additional £5. In Australia and New Zealand, the Tiger Moth was readily adapted to aerial application, using imports, mostly from the UK, offered in pairs, completely rebuilt, at knock-down prices.

The cheap aeroplanes were supported by hundreds of tons of spare parts. Under Air Ministry contracts, de Havillands continued with production of specific spares until 1952, whilst in Australia two enterprising concerns built up a number of Tiger Moths entirely from new 'surplus' parts drawn from their massive stockholding.

Canadian Tiger Moths did not enjoy a new lease of life to the same extent; many were sold for scrap, leaving proportionately fewer under civilian ownership as a tribute to their immensely valuable contribution to aircrew training in North America.

Thousands of words have been written about the Tiger Moth, not all of them kind. Dozens of articles and technical descriptions have appeared in learned journals, popular papers and every publication in between. The aeroplane has been analysed and dissected and immortalised. The Tiger Moth is currently a museum exhibit, a worn out frame symbolising Twenties' technology; at the same instant she is a competition standard aerobatic mount, a prized possession, a financial investment, a toy, an everyday transport of delight, a workhorse. Fifty and more years on she is still the subject of controversial Airworthiness Directives, imaginitive modifications, pilot licence endorsements; yet she can still renew her "commercial" status in a world where the authorities look ever harder for incipient flaws, all in the public interest.

In this book I have attempted to take an alternative view of the Tiger Moth, of her life and times, through the medium of the photograph. The man with the camera had been at readiness for a hundred years and had perfected his art by the time the Tiger Moth made her debut. Not by accident perhaps, a photographer was present on almost every occasion when the lady had something new to show; something fresh to add to her already extensive repertoire.

Acknowledgements

These pictures are the distillation of thousands that have been carefully sifted, sorted, selected and chosen finally to illustrate the life story of a star.

Such a compilation would be impossible without the unselfish support of Tiger Moth devotees from all parts of the world. Inevitably, some who offered the gems of their personal collections will be disappointed not to see their jewels in print. Rejecting pictures of Tiger Moths was the saddest task of all.

Contributions were received from Great Britain, USA, Australia, New Zealand, Canada, France, Germany, Holland, Spain, Denmark, Norway, Finland, South Africa, Switzerland, Hong Kong and Singapore; almost as many countries as those that have included Tiger Moths in their military forces and civil clubs not to mention the legions of those infectiously enthusiastic private owners.

Every submission was valuable and necessary to maintain the momentum, and each package was opened with unsuppressed excitement and anticipation. On occasions, acute disappointment was quickly vanquished by euphoria as pure gold dust spilled onto my desk. I hope some of the unique vibrations generated by the passage of a classic biplane can be sensed through these pages, and you will receive as much pleasure in viewing as I enjoyed whilst selecting.

Unfortunately, it is not possible to list individually the dozens of contributors, but I must make special mention of the following enthusiasts who tolerated my persistence with the patience born of practice and in the knowledge that I wouldn't go away:

Darryl Cott of British Aerospace Civil Aircraft Division, Hatfield; Richard Riding, Editor, *Aeroplane Monthly;* Janic Geelen; Roger Jackson; Reg Bonner; John King and Neville Parnell.

In addition I should like to thank the archivists of the following public institutions who often went beyond the call of reasonable duty when faced only with scant or vague reference:

The Library, Royal Aircraft Establishment Farnborough; Museums of the Royal Air Force; Royal New Zealand Air Force; Australian War Memorial; Fleet Air Arm; Canadian National Aviation and the Science Museum and Imperial War Museum.

Special thanks are due to Michael Vaisey for checking my manuscript, and to my wife Miranda for typing it.

Stuart McKay, Berkhamsted, Hertfordshire.
February 22nd., 1987.

Photographic Acknowledgements

Air Photo Supply 91, 156; Air Portraits 67; AAA Australia 66; The Aeroplane 16, 34, 51, 52, 54, 55; Reg Bonner 37, 140, 149; Adrian Balch 79; John Blake 103; Peter Bish 155; Sue Burges 128, 133; Charles E. Brown 121; Torkild Balslev 137, 158; BL Heritage 36, 46; British Aerospace 9, 20, 23, 24, 25, 28, 30, 31, 35, 36, 42, 45, 48, 65, 88, 96; Tim Carbury 19; John Carter 49; Per Cederqvist 17; Central Press 85; Barry Dowsett 42, 82; Dominion Press 86; Herman Dekker 93; Michael Dressler 157; Richard Dent 118.

Norman Eastaff 146; M. Eltz 26; Fox Photos 2; Ivor Faulconer 143; Fleet Air Arm Museum 90, 142; Flight 10, 11, 12, 14, 22, 29, 32, 33, 41, 50, 87, 89, 106, 107, 111, 127, 132, 134, 135; Geiselhard 21; Janic Geelen 44, 124, 141; Julie Hanks 77; Charles Holland 90, 94; John Hughes 105; Bill Hitchcock 97; Tom Hamill 104; Jerry Hughes 109; Kurt Hofschneider 119; Roger Jackson 13, 43, 56, 62, 81, 96, 101, 108, 109, 131, 154; Mike Jerram 147; Jeremy Johnston 58; Anthony James 153; Keystone 15, 69; John King 130, 148, 150; Adam Keys 60.

Peter le Coyte 80; Ministry of Information 73; Maurice Marsh 104; S. McKnight 76; John Monholf 123; Charles Neal 38; National Aeronautical Collection 42; News of the World 144; Bjorn Olsen 27; P. H. Ogden 61; J. O'Reilly 70; Bill Orbeck 151; Dudley Payne 145; Planet News 115; Cyril Peckham 72; Neville Parnell 66, 95, 100, 122; Photographic News Agencies 68; Norman Pealing 18, 39, 59, 117; Richard Riding 45, 102, 124, 125, 136; Ernest Riley 84; Stan Roberts 94; Hannu Riihela 99; Rothmans 152; Royal Air Force Museum 113; Royal Australian Air Force Museum 116; Royal New Zealand Air Force Museum 47, 53, 71, 74, 75; Royal Aircraft Establishment Farnborough 64.

D. Stirling 63; Starliner Aviation Press 98; Greg Shepherd 120; Stevens and Magielsen 108; Keith Sissons 138; Speed 126; Gerry Schwam 160; V. Trueman 92; Topical Press 112; Dr F. Trevarthen 114; Werner Ulmer 159; Ray Vuillermin 40, 139; R. Wilson 57; Ian Wheeler 83; David Wilkinson 61; Wiltshire Newspapers 110; Alex Weston 129.

1. The Family Tree

Geoffrey de Havilland was designing aeroplanes long before the demise of the Aircraft Manufacturing Company, whose closure precipitated him into joining forces with former colleagues to establish his own company in 1920 at the age of 38.

The de Havilland Aircraft Company Ltd., moved bodily into premises on Stag Lane aerodrome, a stone's thrown from Hendon where "The Captain" as he was reverentially known, had already made a reputation as designer and pilot.

Stag Lane had originated as a Hendon overspill where, in the quiet of the countryside, the London and Provincial Aviation Company trained pilots for the Royal Flying Corps. After the Armistice, the company had attempted to build civil light aeroplanes until they clashed with bureaucracy, lost their battle, diversified, went down again and eventually sold up. But they maintained the freehold on the land.

Business for DH's was slow in common with most others in aviation at that time; work was sufficient only for fragile maintenance of a small but dedicated workforce. In the midst of a cash crisis in October 1921 when the company had been advised that it must buy the Stag Lane freehold or get out, a young sporting pilot, Alan S. Butler, was directed to the DH offices upon the advice of C. G. Grey, perspicacious Editor of *The Aeroplane*.

Alan Butler outlined his specification for a two/three seat racing tourer and asked whether de Havillands could build it. The instinct of the chief designer and his works manager was to quote a ridiculously high price in the hope that this young

The first "private owner" design attempted by de Havillands was to the commission of Alan S. Butler, a wealthy young sportsman, whose £3,000 DH37 built in 1922 helped to save the fledgling company from financial embarrassment.

The DH37 could be flown as a single, two or three seater, and was used extensively as a long distance touring and racing aircraft. In some respects, the design was unusual for the period being a single bay biplane with differential ailerons on the lower wings, supporting a ply covered fuselage.

Too small: built to a specification called up by the Light Aeroplane Trialists at Lympne for the 1923 meeting, the DH53 Humming Bird proved to be too light a light aeroplane for serious and practical use, although some notable and publicity worthy long distance flights were made on behalf of de Havillands by Alan Cobham.

man might pay up or else go away. Not only did Alan Butler agree to pay £3,000 for what became the DH37, but he immediately offered to invest a further £50,000. The offer was accepted and Stag Lane purchased outright. The future was assured. Alan Butler became a director, then Chairman, a post he held for almost thirty years.

DH had frequently considered the specification for a practical light aeroplane which could be offered at a price acceptable to prospective private owners. The de Havilland entry built against the formula published for the 1923 Lympne Light Aeroplane Trials was a pair of DH53 Humming Birds, but they were obviously too small, underpowered and unsuited to serious touring. The Lympne philosophy had failed. DH turned instead to the Type 51, a two/three seat biplane built around cheap war surplus RAF 1A engines. Performance was good but there was a problem with civil certification of the engine, and otherwise the airframe was too big.

Too big: the DH51 was designed around the surplus RAF 1A engine, available according to legend, at less than £1 each. The two bay biplane was DH's reaction to the formula for the Lympne Light Aeroplane Trials, which he considered to be impractical and restrictive; instead he offered a big, strong aeroplane, capable of operation from small fields.

With experience gained from earlier attempts to design a realistically priced and practical private owner aeroplane, Geoffrey de Havilland outlined a new shape on his drawing board at Stag Lane in 1924. The aircraft was to be a two seat biplane built from wood and powered by a cheap and reliable Cirrus engine, developing 60 horse power. There would be petrol sufficient for over 300 miles range at a cruising speed of 80 mph, and ample baggage space for a couple intending to spend a weekend away. A cockpit operated hand starter was a novelty although there were no parking or taxi brakes. Differential ailerons were to be fitted to the lower mainplanes only, and the aircraft would be stressed for aerobatics. For easy garaging, the wings would fold back against the fuselage.

On February 22nd 1925 the little biplane spread her clear doped wings and in the hands of her designer flew into the North London sky. It was Sunday afternoon.

Geoffrey de Havilland insisted on a name rather than a mere type number for his new creation, and in deference to his lifelong interest in entomology the Company Board agreed to his own suggestion: "Moth".

De Havillands were always quick to seize on product feedback generated by agents and operators. The initial wooden Moth construction gave way to steel tube fuselage frames, Gipsy series engines with their lowered thrust line and consequently improved view for the pilot, steerable tailskids and split undercarriage systems.

Anticipating a designated trainer version of the developed DH60M Metal Moth, de Havillands offered the DH60T Moth Trainer in 1931. Primarily for military use, the aircraft could be fitted with practice bombs, camera guns, wireless and reconnaissance equipment.

To cope with a multi-role operation, the airframe was strengthened; the wing structure was revised incorporating a new airfoil section and gross weight increased by 600 lb compared with the first prototype.

This 1940 shot of an operational Tiger Moth serves to illustrate how she won her stripes. Clearly visible is the forward location of the flying wire attachment lug, leaving the walkway clear for the occupant of the front seat. By moving the centre section and fuel tank forward of the front cockpit, upward visibility was improved and the emergency escape path cleared. Sweeping the wings compensated for the forward shift in centre of gravity, simply yet effectively, at the same time creating a unique planform.

Experience of practical requirements led directly to the DH60 of February 1925. The aeroplane was an instant success; it was the right size, carried pilot and passenger quickly and economically, was relatively inexpensive to buy and maintain, and the wings could be folded back for accommodation in a DH inspired "garage". The aeroplane was called Moth.

At first, only wooden Moths were built and with increased demand the selling prices were reduced. Overseas commitments soon identified the need for a Moth with a steel tube fuselage frame, and the resulting DH60M Metal Moth was introduced in 1928. Three years later, whilst complying with a military specification, a DH60M had been so extensively modified that it was re-designated DH60T Moth Trainer. Powered by the Gipsy II engine, the DH60T fulfilled export orders from Sweden, China, Egypt, Brazil and Iraq.

Modifying and inverting the basic Gipsy engine for installation in an airframe which ultimately became the Puss Moth, resulted in the Gipsy III. This new powerplant was fitted to a DH60T and offered against an Air Ministry specification for a new RAF trainer. This called amongst other needs, for better escape prospects for the parachute encumbered instructor, usually surrounded in his front cockpit by an entanglement of wires and struts.

Stag Lane legend has it that a DH60T was incarcerated in an isolated shed where the centre section was repositioned forward of the front cockpit, and to compensate for the consequent shift in centre of gravity, all four wings were swept backwards by the simple expedient of cutting off the rear spar root ends with a handsaw. Later, when it was required that the CG should be moved even further rearward, the top wings only were re-set, in the interests of spar economy on the prototype it has been suggested.

To tidy the paperwork, the DH60T, now named Tiger Moth to correspond with the "T" in her designation, was redefined by her makers as the DH Type 82. The family tree had established another branch and there were to be many more before the Stag Lane sapling blossomed into full maturity.

The legend is born. Conversion of a DH60T into a DH60T Tiger Moth was accomplished in a Stag Lane shed with the aid of saws, drills and calculations on the backs of old envelopes. At least, that is the way popular myth would have us believe, although it may not be far from the truth.

In September 1931, the first of two prototypes of the DH60T Tiger Moth, G-ABNJ, was tested at Martlesham Heath under the DH Class 2 markings E.5. The recommendation that increased dihedral on the lower wings would prevent the ailerons from touching the ground whilst taxying was incorporated into the second test aircraft G-ABPH, and at the same time the opportunity was taken to increase the sweep on the top mainplanes. DH considered that such changes constituted a major departure from the basic DH60 theme, and elected to issue a new Type number. Following the disappointment of the Swallow Moth, Type Number DH81, the de Havilland Company hoped to fare better with their next series allocation.

On October 26th 1931, G-ABRC/E6, the first aircraft built specifically as a Type DH82, was flown from Stag Lane by Hubert Broad, a historic event unrecorded in his log book.

DH82 Tiger Moth K2570 was one of the first batch of Gipsy III powered aircraft ordered under Air Ministry contract 120255.

The 1931 Tiger Moths were painted in the standard RAF colour scheme of the day: aluminium overall with the red, white and blue rudder stripes prominently displayed. It was a time when manufacturers were still permitted to apply trade marks, and K2570 wore the characteristic DH symbol on each face of the four interplane struts.

2. Early Days

In 1931 the Type 82 was vying for the attention of the Air Ministry. The de Havilland Aircraft Company had high hopes that its new basic trainer would easily satisfy the scrutineers of the Experimental Establishment at Martlesham Heath, after which a production contract might be offered.

Following intensive evaluation and competition, the Stag Lane design was accepted, subject to modification, and an initial order for 35 aircraft was agreed.

The first batch of military Tiger Moths was comprehensively air tested overhead Stag Lane in November 1931 much to the general satisfaction of the DH workforce, and the following day the aeroplanes were ferried to RAF Grantham. The pilots of No. 24 (Communications) Squadron, normally based at Northolt, described the generous pre-departure hospitality as "typically DH" and welcome in view of the sub-zero temperature.

Until 1933 when an improved version of the Tiger Moth was built (the Gipsy Major powered DH82A), production at Stag Lane concentrated on successive RAF orders in addition to satisfying contracts for the Reserve Flying Schools and overseas bookings from as far afield as Japan, Persia and Brazil. In marked contrast to the expansive campaigns which resulted in hundreds of civilian DH60 Moths being sold throughout the world, only seven DH82s were released to non-military

The appeal of the Tiger Moth has been unrivalled for fifty years, upstaging even the Hawker biplanes during their reign of superiority in the Thirties.

Empire Air Day 1935, and No 24 (Communications) Squadron plays host to the public at Hendon aerodrome. Under the watchful eye of a beribboned RAF sergeant and two airmen, London schoolboys are permitted to push, pull and poke. An unusually lenient attitude on the part of the Royal Air Force perhaps, even for 1935, but what magic for the school-capped youngsters: the aura of a real aeroplane, the touch, the smell, the view of the cockpit's depths. By the time the peace faded in 1939, several of the boys in this picture might well have exchanged their caps for flying helmets, and were getting to know the Tiger Moth even more intimately.

Flt. Lt. Charles Turner-Hughes (TocH to his contemporaries) on tour, somewhere in England, in 1932.
In a single season with Alan Cobham's National Aviation Day Display, Charles Turner-Hughes recorded these extraordinary statistics on a Tiger Moth:
780 hours flying of which 176 hours were inverted; 2,328 loops, 2,190 rolls, 567 bunts, 522 upward rolls, 40 inverted falling leaf manoeuvres and 5 outside loops.
G-ABUL was impressed into military service at Sywell in September 1940 and used for initial training until June 1944. Whilst engaged on a low flying exercise, the aircraft collided with a cyclist and crashed, to be damaged beyond repair.

customers in the home country, and most of those joined one or other of the famous travelling Air Displays.

The success of the uprated DH82A resulted in a flood of Air Ministry and export orders which kept the DH production line (transferred to Hatfield after the closure of Stag Lane) fully occupied until 1937. Only then were contracts negotiated to supply civil flying clubs wishing to re-equip, but the days of peace were already numbered.

The flow of civil aircraft had been progressing steadily until all production was geared once more solely to military demands. Had the world not embroiled itself in conflict for six years, one wonders just how many Tigers Moths might have rolled from Hatfield's factory. Would the aeroplane have been an exclusive product of Great Britain, built in limited hundreds, or would she still have stamped her personality on the world's training organisations, flying under a greater collection of national flags than anybody could have imagined?

A feature of UK light aviation pre-war was the involvement of the Automobile Association who not only provided maps and charts and an en-route service, but AA "scouts" who attended flying meetings. Their routine included picketing and covering of aircraft, assistance with fuelling and starting, chocking and checking that pilot, passenger and aeroplane were ready for departure.
These two DH82s belonged to the Bristol School. The long exhaust pipes were a fairly familiar sight on early Tiger Moths operating in areas where even in 1932, complaints about noise were voiced.

Pre-war, the Royal Swedish Air Force operated British and Swedish built DH82s and locally manufactured DH82As under the local designation Sk.11 and Sk.11A.

The colour scheme was not only cheerful, displaying a nationalistic rudder stripe, but highly visual in the event of a forced landing amongst the trees in summer or the snowfields in winter. At least one Swedish military Sk.11A operated on floats from the Vasteras Centrala Flygverkstaden (CVV) at which establishment was built, between 1939 and 1945, the Sk.12, better known as the German equivalent of the Tiger Moth, the Focke Wulf Steiglitz.

This photograph was taken in April 1985 following restoration by Per Cederqvist of British built Tiger Moth 3364, a Hatfield product of 1935. The aircraft was allocated to the de Havilland administered No 13 EFTS at White Waltham as G-ADLV and retained those markings until October 1940 when she was impressed as BB750. The aeroplane remained in active service with a number of RAF units until October 1953 when she was sold into civilian hands and incorrectly registered G-AORA. She became SE-CWG in July 1963 and wears that registration now, together with anti-spin strakes which neither Sk.11 nor Sk.11A ever did.

At the outbreak of war, Swedish Air Force training aircraft adopted a near black fuselage with dark orange wings and empennage. Nothing could have been more different from the bright days of peace.

A dramatic pose by a Tiger Moth held for an instant by the camera, looking just like a scale model suspended under a cotton wool skyscape. The colour scheme could identify the aeroplane as one from a number of pre-war clubs or schools. Yellow is a particularly good Tiger Moth colour, set off by silvered wings, and is just as popular half a century into the aeroplane's career.

Blue is not a colour usually associated with Tiger Moths, although many DH60 Moths appeared fresh from Stag Lane's paintshop in a particular shade known throughout the industry as de Havilland blue.
This full-span registration was originally allocated to a 1939 Piper Cub Coupé, but the war intervened. Having never been carried, the letters were re-allocated 40 years later to lend a period flavour to a neat restoration.

During thirty working years, thousands of Tiger Moths flew hundreds of thousands of circuits training two distinct generations of pilots. Now, in the hands of the enthusiasts, mere hundreds of aeroplanes are worked cautiously, flying when the weather is right; on an occasion of significance, or for a training run with the owner's grandson!

Getting a Tiger Moth down onto the grass in a three point attitude when the wind is from the port side, is an art that will never be lost, although it might take greater application.

The engine revs are the same, the airspeed and attitude identical to that taught when the Tiger was young. The concentration of pilot and passenger will always be acute, willing those boots to grease onto the grass.

In March 1933 de Havillands announced their improved version of the
DH82: with a ply rear decking, front and rear doors of equal depth and a
Gipsy Major engine, the standard production variant became the DH82A,
or in RAF nomenclature, the Tiger Moth Mk II.
In sixteen months, 114 DH82s had been built at Stag Lane and Hatfield,
three in Sweden, 17 in Norway plus one constructed by students of the de
Havilland Aeronautical Technical School.
Company demonstrator G-ACJA was operational from August 1933 and
the following April represented DH at the Geneva Aero Show in
company with a locally registered DH60 and a Leopard Moth. Following
precedent, the Tiger Moth was sold five months later to an undisclosed
export customer, believed to be Persia.

Geoffrey Tyson filled the slot in the National Aviation Day routine after Turner-Hughes' departure, and DH82A G-ACEZ was added to Alan Cobham's fleet.

Always searching for new and breathtaking routines with which to stun the crowd, Geoffrey Tyson fitted a spike to the tip bow of the port lower wing and during the 1934-36 flying seasons, picked a handkerchief off the ground on more than 800 occasions.

Apart from the entertainment, the skill of the pilot and a superb demonstration of the safe, slow flying capabilities of the Tiger Moth were evident; a splendid advertisement for the products of Alan Cobham's former employer.

In full view of the housing line that was soon to sweep down the hill and engulf Stag Lane aerodrome, a production DH82 awaits delivery to the Deutchen Reichsverkehrs Minestekion. The aircraft was built towards the end of the DH82 run, when de Havillands were already working on advanced plans to install the Gipsy Major engine and make other modifications prior to a designation change.

This photograph offers a clear view of the blind flying hood, used to cover the pupil's cockpit, and under which the trainee pilot could fly on instruments from take off to rejoin. The trailing edge of the hood was attached to the ply decking by a row of turn studs and the supporting framework overlapped the square-cut doors which could not be opened whenever the device was carried.

In the publicity material reflecting the glories of their Tiger Moth as an all purpose military aeroplane, the DH copywriters promoted the following:

The Tiger Moth fulfils all primary, intermediate and advanced training requirements. It exhibits the characteristics of the high powered, high performance types in which pupils will ultimately fly, yet it is economical both in first cost and upkeep. For the training and exercise of fighting the Tiger Moth is equipped with a camera gun. As a two seater observation or reconnaissance aircraft it carries wireless telegraphy apparatus and camera equipment. As a long range light bomber a bomb rack is fitted carrying 4 x 20lb practise bombs.

A testing disc, used to set the Pratt and Whitney synchronising gear, established that gun firing was safe between engine speeds of 800 and 2,400 rpm.

What DH did not spell out in their 1932 advertisement was the fact that "a foreign government" had commissioned a Tiger Moth fighter aircraft, in which the camera gun was augmented by a Czech built machine gun of .92 mm calibre, firing up to 900 rounds per minute through the propeller arc. The gun could be removed, thus returning the aircraft to a standard training configuration.

The "fighter" was unveiled in October 1933, and the press speculated that the aircraft was probably intended for ground strafing rather than aerial duelling. It is believed that 30 Tiger Moth fighters were built and the export customer was later identified as the government of Persia.

This Austrian Tiger Moth is pictured flying over the Alps, probably
during delivery early in 1937. In her particular production batch aircraft
were built for customers in India, South Africa, Iraq, Rhodesia, Ceylon,
Lithuania and the UK's influential Brooklands Flying Club.
OE-DIK is being flown in the single seat configuration and might have
been used for glider tugging. When the Germans occupied Austria, a
number of Tiger Moths was taken over by the military and impressed as
trainers. They were scrapped only after the spares ran out.

In November 1933 the Norwegian Ministry of Defence approved the purchase of a set of floats from Short Bros. of Rochester. These were fitted to Army Tiger Moth "159" which was test flown for a total of 21 hours and 40 minutes on behalf of the Naval Air Service. The trials were conducted at Karljohansvaern from February 14th 1934 after which the Navy decided the Tiger Moth on floats was not suited to its purpose. This view coincided with a similar assessment drawn up by the Royal Air Force after experimenting with a pair of float equipped aircraft.

At the time the Norwegian trials' aircraft was due to be returned to the Army airfield at Kjeller, the Navy was notified that the aerodrome was flooded, a situation which permitted the flying return of "159" whilst still attached to the float undercarriage.

During the next six years, Tiger Moth "159" logged about 100 hours per year, until May 6th 1940 when in company with others, she flew to northern Norway to continue the struggle against the invaders. Immediately after the capitulation, the aircraft flew under false civil markings to Finland, where she was accepted into service with the Finnish Air Force. Minor damage was caused on May 17th 1944 during a forced landing due to engine failure, but the aircraft was not repaired. The dismantled Tiger Moth was stored for four years and eventually broken up in 1948.

When the London Aeroplane Club was formed at Stag Lane in August 1925, it did so around the first DH60 Moths, and was responsible to the Royal Aero Club and the Air Ministry, both of whom had an interest. Stag Lane aerodrome offered excellent facilities for Club members and private owners, but the pressures exerted by the expansion of suburbia caused de Havillands to establish in 1930, a new factory site at Hatfield. The works gradually transferred until the closure of Stag Lane aerodrome in July 1934, but the London Aeroplane Club had moved overnight in September 1933, at which point the constitution of the Club was changed. The London Aeroplane Club was taken under the wing of the de Havilland Aircraft Company and used as the primary source of subsidised flying for employees. The old de Havilland School of Flying which had enjoyed a joint civil/military role, became a Reserve and Elementary Flying Training School operating Tiger Moths, although some Jaguar-engined DH9Js were retained initally.

This picture, probably taken in September 1938, illustrates the time-honoured method for one-man-manoeuvring of a Tiger Moth, which explains why pre-war engineers were all broad shouldered. We trust that the parachute packing pilot is not actually pushing on the port aileron, but rather checking the wingtip clearance.

Parked on the airfield is a DH93 Don and an example of the beautiful wooden DH91 Albatross airliner. The Don was crippled by its own specification, the Albatross programme was curtailed by the war, and the whole of the LAC Tiger Moth fleet joined the Royal New Zealand Air Force in December 1939.

A pleasing and classical shot of a pre-war civil Tiger Moth: G-AESD of
the Brooklands Flying Club. The aeroplane was registered in March 1937
at a time when orders for new aircraft were being quickly satisfied and
before accelerated production was called up to cope with an entirely
military demand.

Like so many others, G-AESD was requisitioned and allocated a military
serial, BD156, in August 1940. Having led a short but energetic life at
Brooklands aerodrome, fate was cruel: BD156 was not destined to beat
the circuit training another generation of pilots; she was placed in storage
then allocated as an instructional airframe until scrapped in February
1945.

At least 30 Tiger Moths parked outside the final assembly shops at
Hatfield on September 26th 1935, await distribution to the Reserve
Schools. Some are for the home team where delivery required a two
hundred yard taxi; others were scheduled for the DH establishment at
White Waltham and their near neighbours at Woodley.

Those which survived into mid 1940 lost their civilian coats and were
issued military serials and dulled camouflage suits of brown and green.
The fleets were gradually dispersed within the myriad requirements of
service postings until 1945 when the old stalwarts found their way to
pastures new, often foreign fields, or were ungraciously allocated to the
scrap bins.

Although civilian operated, the old de Havilland School of Flying was always a Reserve unit, and as No. 1 EFTS based at Hatfield, used a fleet of Tiger Moths built a few hundred yards from its own Headquarters. The instructors wore a military style uniform supplied by DH until most became Reserve officers in their own right, and adopted full RAF kit. Clem Pike (standing right), was appointed CFI of the Hatfield base after Bob Reeve had moved to White Waltham to take command of the new school established there as part of the Expansion Programme in 1935. The shot of Tiger Moth G-ACDG and the two instructors was taken at Hatfield on January 24th 1939. The aeroplane is camouflaged but carries civil letters. The outer panels of the top wings are yellow, in unison with the elevator; the interim between full civil and full military.

G-ACDG was impressed in 1940 and remained at Hatfield until 1941 when a landing accident routed her to a civil repair organization. There followed a number of accidents with various units, repairs and storage, reallocation of her civil letters for a spell with Vosper shipbuilders in 1944, and eventual sale to a flying school at Cambridge in 1946 where she gave the first post-war civil flying lesson. A year later she was in Holland, fitted with a hideous Fokker fin, teaching new pilots at the National Flying School.

December 1935: the RAF Expansion Programme gathers momentum. Complete with factory new flying kit and Tiger Moths, these pupil pilots were amongst the first to report to the Reid and Sigrist School at Desford, where they paraded for the press during a ministerial visit.

3. To make a Moth

Initially, Tiger Moths were built at de Havilland's Stag Lane factory, taking their place on the assembly shop floor with a mix of late development DH60s, Puss, Fox, Leopard and Hornet Moths, Dragon, Dragon Rapide and the redoubtable DH86.

By the time Stag Lane had closed to flying in July 1934, the new aerodrome and factory complex at Hatfield was fully operational, supporting the Moth equipped London Aeroplane Club and de Havilland Reserve School.

Here too, the assembly shops played host to a variety of different designs but with the ever increasing prospect of war, the Tiger Moth took the ascendancy and production was accelerated.

With the exciting new Mosquito ordered into full production yet the continuing and increasing need for still more Tiger Moths, there developed an inevitable conflict in the allocation of resources. In 1940, the Ministry of Aircraft Production decided to transfer all UK Tiger Moth manufacture into the hands of the motor industry. Morris Motors was contracted to establish a line at Cowley near Oxford,

de Havillands built DH82 and 82A Tiger Moths at Stag Lane and Hatfield between 1931 and 1940 after which all production was transferred to Morris Motors at Cowley.

The Hatfield assembly shops were full of airframes in March 1939 when his photograph was taken, as increased military orders were fulfilled. The Gipsy Major engines came from Stag Lane, where factory floorspace was retained by the de Havilland Engine Company until well into the jet age.

More than twenty Tiger Moth fuselages stand in line. Paint marks on the concrete floor establish the ordered dressing, vital for mass production when factory space is at a premium.

Production details were chalked onto the front fuselage bulkhead or the forward top decking of each individual aircraft. Note the dent in the oil tank of the most completely visible fuselage. In service this would soon be joined by others as mechanics used the tank as a step to reach the petrol supply.

absorbing a number of incomplete Hatfield supplied airframes with which to plot their learning curve.

Alongside military vehicle construction, Morris Motors quickly organised an assembly track for Tiger Moth fuselages which progressed through tunnel type surroundings under the influence of a chain link drive. This typical mass production style was later changed and relocated in more spacious premises where fuselages were built on individual dollies; hand propelled along guide rails to the next stage in their development.

Nearly all components used at Cowley were made in-house although some wooden parts were supplied by outside contractors, crudely nailed and glued perhaps, products of the nation's cottage industrialisation. Engines, instruments, electrics, wheels, tyres and propellers were bought in to take their allotted places on the airframes, assembled almost exclusively by female labour.

The longevity of the Tiger Moth owes much to its unit construction: the fuselage is simply a pair of tubular side frames lying in parallel, tied together by two cross frames and a rear pylon. Add a simple ply floor, a trio of wooden top deckings and two engine bearers, and one has a basic fuselage. The undercarriage, centre section, fin and tailplane bolt to the fuselage; four wooden wings are braced by streamlined wires; the engine sits between two square tube frames, close cowled, whilst levers and brackets, pulleys and guides, seats and instruments each locate in predetermined pickup points. Bend a part, even a major component, and the

Once final assembly was initiated, substantially more floor area was required per aircraft, and stacking of mainplanes and control surfaces was monitored by production engineers.

This Hatfield batch was photographed on April 16th 1939. The aircraft nearest the camera is a Queen Bee, identified by the covered rear cockpit and sling wires attached to the centre section. Less obvious is the fact that the fuselage is made of wood, based on the DH60GIII Moth Major design.

Alongside the Queen Bee is a Tiger Moth trainer destined for the Persian Air Force. This has not taken advantage of the reprofiled rear door, an RAF inspired modification which permitted the doors to be opened even when a blind flying hood was attached.

Third aircraft in the line is RAF Tiger Moth N-6728, beyond which the remaining six aircraft all appear to be standard RAF issue.

Early summer 1939, Tiger Moth N-6852, fresh from the paintshop, and wearing a period camouflage scheme which included bright yellow outer wing panels and empennage, is under the care and attention of the Aerodrome Engineer's Staff at Hatfield.
Whilst the engine is running, the intrepid mechanic is holding a vibration gauge against the crankcase top cover. The helmet and goggles are an essential part of the ritual which had been practised hundreds of times already in preparation for the thousands yet to come.

repair is effective and simple: release the damaged section and bolt on a spare.

In Australia and New Zealand, wartime Tiger Moth production was initiated by the de Havilland overseas companies using UK manufactured parts prior to total conversion to home produced items. Minor modifications considered necessary in view of the operating environment or as basic improvements to an otherwise rustic structure, were incorporated on local demand.

de Havilland Canada was not enthusiastic about the Tiger Moth demonstrator sent from England in 1936, even after fitting a canopy in a vain attempt to keep winter at bay. The aeroplane was therefore, "re-designed"; RCAF requirements and experience gained by the local operation of DH60Ms were considered. The British aeroplane was dismantled and each part used to make patterns and jigs for a production version known as the DH82A (Can). Further refinements late in 1939 attracted the company designation DH82C, the ultimate basic Tiger Moth, perhaps.

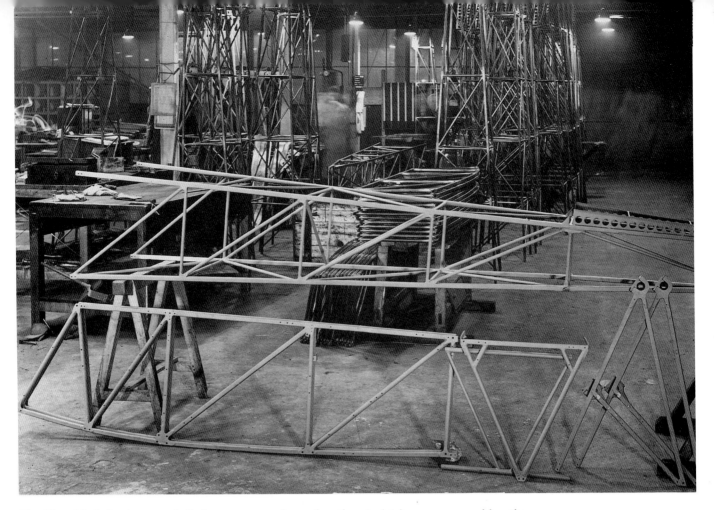

The Tiger Moth fuselage was built from square and round section steel tube; pre-prepared lengths welded together in jigs to become frames. The basic fuselage structure was easy to design and stress; easy to assemble from a miscellany of components; easy to dismantle for storage and easy to repair in the event of damage. All major components were located at pre-drilled points: engine bearers, undercarriage, mainplanes, centre section, top deckings and floor.

The control box bolts to the floor complete with rear rudder bar, sticks and associated linkages, cross bracing tubes and seat supports. The floor bolts directly to the front frames. Without question, the simplicity of the design and construction of the Tiger Moth fuselage is the principal reason for the longevity of the type, even considering the thirteen years of continuous production and the massive spares provisioning that supported 8,000 aeroplanes in the field.

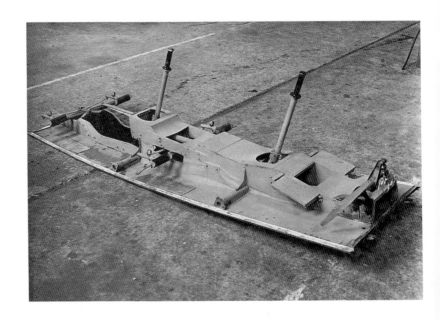

It looks like a Moth. It flies like a Moth. It sounds like a Moth. It feels like a Moth. And the graphic artist who designed the colour scheme was attempting to keep it that way.

Built as L-6938 for the RAF in 1937, the aeroplane was civilianised in 1955 and written off as 'damaged beyond economical repair' in 1970. But that was 1970. The age of the enthusiastic amateur restorer who spends years working against no pay, has since broken into full bloom. For ten years this once discarded wreckage has been a starter at every UK aerobatic event organised with Tiger Moths in mind.

Overleaf: One can sense the pilot willing this Tiger Moth to fly sweetly past the assembled company. One can feel the urgency in the Tiger's attitude, wanting to put up a good show.

Late lamented Neil Williams with red and white Tiger Moth in classic pose before the display crowd at Old Warden.

The delightful symmetry is disturbed only by the untidy style of the registration letters, but this and much else was altered after the aeroplane spun into the ground at Old Warden some years later and was severely damaged.

The pilot reported engine failure during an overshoot on a trajectory which might have taken him through the roof of the museum. To turn at low airspeed he knew could be fatal. Faced with a split second decision he booted in the rudder. Result: the museum remains in business, the aeroplane's registration letters have been re-positioned and the pilot's dentist amended his records.

The closure of Croydon airport deprived the demilitarised UK Tiger Moth of its natural habitat. The last of the major overhaul agencies, Rollason Aircraft and Engines, split much of its remaining properties between Rochester and Fairoaks, casting excess stock items considered to be of low relative value, to a melancholy bonfire.

An eventual change of management at Fairoaks resulted in the Rollason caravan taking to the road again, headed to Shoreham where engine and airframe facilities were consolidated. The last Tiger Moth to have been rebuilt at Fairoaks was G-AXBZ, an ex-military export/import via French aero clubs for whom she had tugged gliders. Having used many of the last ''brand new'' spares held in stock, G-AXBZ was sold to the same two co-owners who had contracted in turn for the previous pair of Fairoaks rebuilt Tiger Moths, and who considered that G-AXBZ at the time, was probably the finest original example of a DH82A anywhere in the world.

Built at Mascot in 1943, Tiger Moth A17-656 accrued only 314 hours with the RAAF before sale. Her early civilian owners included Pastoral Services (Duttons) who personalised her registration as VH-PSD, although surprisingly she never was pressed into agricultural service. VH-PSD was rebuilt by a consortium in 1974 and six years later sold to new owner John Petit, to supplement the DH80, DH87A and DH87B in his collection.

In over 40 years, VH-PSD has logged only 1,130 hours total time, including that during this photographic session at Kyneton, Victoria, when Ray Vuillermin took his hands off the controls and entrusted the landing to the crouching occupant of the front cockpit.

The hard leading edges, unique to Australian Moth wings, are clearly visible in this shot.

When UK Tiger Moth production was switched to Morris Motors at Cowley early in 1940, the first aircraft were assembled on link driven production lines using parts supplied by de Havillands.

Running in parallel with military vehicle manufacture, the motor industry attempted to apply the same techniques to light aeroplane construction, and a sour atmosphere developed between the Morris management and resident DH technical representatives concerning the quality of some of the early aircraft.

Using a DH built fuselage as a pattern, Morris completed their first Tiger Moth in April 1940. The aircraft was taken by road to Hatfield for a thorough inspection where 67 major complaints were listed, although Morris countered by arguing that the aeroplane had been built to Hatfield supplied drawings.

The aircraft was returned to Morris for rectification and eventually taken by road to Witney aerodrome for its first flight. Subsequent Cowley aeroplanes were flown out of a small field behind the assembly shops.

At their Mascot factory between May 1940 and January 1945, de Havilland Australia assembled and later built from self-generated component parts, more than 1,000 Tiger Moths.

In excess of 700 aircraft were taken on charge by the RAAF, but 358 others were delivered to Burma, India, The Netherlands East Indies, New Zealand, South Africa and Rhodesia, one to the Broken Hill Aero Club and an uncertain number, thought to be at least forty-five, to the USAAF in Australia.

Initially, the aircraft were painted yellow with vertical rudder stripes, but there were to be numerous local changes before the Tiger Moth's Service career came finally to an end.

The crates listed at 2 tons 3 cwt on the parked lorries contain dismantled Tiger Moths waiting shipment to Batavia for delivery to the N.I.L.F. (Netherlands Indies Aviation Fund), a government-sponsored organisation whose aircraft were distributed throughout the colony to provide flying training for potential military pilots.

Following delivery to the N.I.L.F. of four second-hand Tiger Moths from England in August 1940, a quartet of new aircraft was ordered from DH Australia, a gift from the rulers of Koeantan and Indragiri.

The new aircraft were assembled at Soerabaja in October 1940 and put into service on November 23rd. One of these, PK-SBF *Koeantan*, was released to the Djocja Flying Club on December 15th at a ceremony attended by the Sultan of Djokjakarta and Prince Pakoe Alam.

It is probable that PK-SBF was one of a large number of Tiger Moths assembled at Tasik Malaja towards the end of the war with the aim of returning the aircraft to Australia. However, the plan was thwarted by the immediate lack of shipping space, and the entire fleet was demolished to prevent the aircraft from falling into enemy hands.

The first twenty Tiger Moths to roll out of the DHA Mascot factory were assembled using imported British fuselages mated with locally built wings. Thereafter all DHA production utilised Australian made components and incorporated many practical modifications which surprisingly were never applied to standard aircraft coming off the lines elsewhere.

The continued RAAF demand for Tiger Moths resulted in the decision to build Gipsy Major engines in Australia rather than to continue importing from the UK, but before production could begin more than 41,000 dimensional conversions were necessary to change de Havilland's metric based drawings into essentially required Imperial units. In July 1940, only seven months after receiving the plans, General Motors-Holdens Ltd were running their first engine on the test bench, and during the next four years delivered 1,300 units.

A17-565 was the one thousandth Tiger Moth to roll off the line at Mascot, a total Australian product, wearing a considerably toned down colour scheme when compared with the radiance of earlier models. This aeroplane is currently alive and well and living in Switzerland.

Before the start of the Second World War, the New Zealand Government suggested that de Havillands should consider domestic production of 100 Tiger Moths for the RNZAF.

In April 1939, Hugh Buckingham was sent from Hatfield to supervise the birth of de Havilland (New Zealand) and a factory site was developed at Rongotai near Wellington, with workshop accommodation reminiscent of any European aircraft production centre dating from the First World War. The promised 100 Tiger Moth contract was signed in August 1939 and required that deliveries should be completed within 18 months at a total cost of £155,000.

Before the factory was complete, 12 aircraft were assembled from parts imported from Hatfield, and these were supplemented by 92 others sent from the UK in dismantled state, for erection, test flying and delivery to the Air Force as part of the Empire Air Training Scheme.

The flow of Hatfield and later Australian built fuselages rigged with locally produced wings gradually gave way to a line of one hundred percent local manufacture, NZ799 being the first original product early in 1941. Wheels, tyres, engines and instruments were still delivered from the UK and most raw materials had to be imported. Including the early assembly jobs, the Rongotai factory eventually turned out 344 Tiger Moths for the RNZAF, many of which went on to distinguished post war careers in civil aviation. Even the factory was converted to an airline passenger terminal.

Not satisfied with the basic DH82 that was sent for evaluation by Hatfield, de Havilland Canada redesigned the aircraft using most of the original components.

The undercarriage was raked forward to improve the chances against tipping the aeroplane onto its nose when the new mainwheel brakes were applied. A heavy duty tailwheel was fitted instead of the basic steel skid, and the elevators were modified to accept a trim tab in preference to the simple spring bias in the cable circuit.

A redesigned cowling was introduced, hinged along the top centreline to allow easier access to the Gipsy Major; steel interplane struts were chosen in spite of the local lumber industry, and the cockpits were modified to accommodate an effective canopy, new instrument layout, and a heating system tapped off the exhaust.

More than 1,500 DH82C Tiger Moths were built by de Havillands in Toronto. Production stopped in 1942 as the factory space was gradually taken over by more urgently needed Ansons and Mosquitos.

The design of the DH82C's canopy permitted operations with the three section lid closed, the front section pulled back to coincide with the rear cockpit, or with both sections slipped back to a position behind the rear seat. It was possible to fly the aircraft with all the sliding parts removed.

Visible in the canopy close-up are the instrument panels, surrounded with thick foam rubber acting as crash pads and fitted in preference to the usual head-roll. A curtain like blind flying hood attached simply to the rear section.

The canopy and the cockpit heater were as inevitable as the extremes of climate they sought to exclude, and a further refinement dictated by cold was the oil tank lagging, for there was no accommodation for the tank inside the fuselage or under the cowlings.

Prior to flight a number of checks were required to be completed by the inspection department: propeller tracking, fuel systems proved against leaks, petrol flow rates calculated. In 1944 at Cowley some of the last production Tiger Moths are progressed through the checklists. Note the extensive camouflage applied to the buildings: dummy windows, doors and infill designed to change the outline of an otherwise obvious factory silhouette.

Following C of G checks, Tiger Moths were flown out of a small field behind the production shops at Cowley, yet a field large enough to permit the operation of Dominies and Spitfires. The Spitfires were routed through Cowley for repair and the Dominie and occasional Proctor acted as taxis for the ferry pilots.

Six before lunch! Production test pilot John Neave is assisted with parachute adjustment at DH New Zealand's production unit at Rongotai, Wellington in 1943, prior to making another series of pre-delivery test flights.

John Neave's long leather coat is evidently not tailored to accommodate the parachute although it would have offered excellent protection when flying open cockpit aircraft.

These Tiger Moths appear to have a locally applied appendage to the lower centre section which might be a mirror, a theory supported by the absence of a similar device set traditionally on one of the port centre section struts.

After building and testing, aeroplanes required delivery to their operational base or distribution centre. The Air Transport Auxiliary was formed in September 1939 to provide a pool of civilian pilots whose responsibility it was to move aircraft from factory to Service establishment, and from operational base to Maintenance Unit, thus releasing Service pilots for other tasks.

No 5 Ferry Pilot Pool was established at Hatfield, and against a backdrop of Tiger Moths awaiting delivery, the ladies of the Pool were introduced to the press on January 10th 1940. Sidcot suits and boots were standard issue, but the ladies obviously had an affection for their own helmets, goggles and gloves, for each was an experienced pre-war pilot.

By the end of the war some of the ladies of ATA were qualified to fly four-engined bombers and transports in addition to the highest performance fighter aircraft of the day.

4. Called to the Colours

A vivid splash of colour radiated from the Hatfield paintshops in July 1936 when official policy decreed that all RAF training aircraft should henceforth, be painted yellow overall. The supply of Tiger Moths to the Reserve Schools resulted in further highly individualistic colour choices until such times that the brown and green of European camouflage was adopted as standard. With minor amendments, all future UK production was finished in these drab tones until the last aeroplane left the Cowley plant in 1944.

From the earliest military aeroplanes, colour schemes have been functional, either highlighting the outline of the aircraft or alternatively attempting to disguise the machine, hiding it from sight for as long as possible in the air or on the ground.

Almost inevitably, and especially at a time when pilots often flew an individual aeroplane, local paint scheme modifications were applied in the field, coloured by location of base perhaps or the whim of a particular commander.

The Tiger Moth had joined the RAF in 1931 as a basic trainer and communications aeroplane, but almost immediately, she adopted an original colour scheme and was heavily modified in order to become latest equipment for the Central Flying School's Formation Aerobatic Team. Forever after, adaptability was to be the watchword in her life.

This scramble was at Elmdon, Birmingham, early in 1940, when trainee Royal Navy pilots, with and without helmets or parachutes, were photographed running towards Tiger Moths of No 14 EFTS, and three hastily impressed and camouflaged civilian Dragon Rapides.
The Tiger Moths reflect the period of changeover from the pre-war military camouflage to 1940 style and the application of individual unit identification by letter or number is evident. The "gas patch", an 18 inch square of green paint which would change colour in the presence of gas is clearly visible on the rear decking of N-5454, which in common with all other Tiger Moths in this picture, has no fin stripes.
The Dragon Rapide at far right, G-AFEO, took up military marks in March 1940 and was abandoned in France the following June.

On a rainy September day in 1938, two Hatfield engineers attach a plumb-bob to the sternpost of a Tiger Moth in preparation for a rigging check.

The aircraft is painted in an early camouflage scheme showing clearly the yellow tip panels, interplane struts, fin, rudder and elevators. The tailplane was camouflaged, but all undersurfaces were yellow.

In the UK she flew wartime coastal patrols searching for submarines at dawn; she carried bombs during the invasion scare and as a result was branded as unco-operative in the matter of recovery from spins. The series of intensive trials at Boscombe Down and Farnborough resulted in the infamous Mod.112, a subject of continuing controversy more than forty years later.

The Tiger Moth served with the Expeditionary Forces in France during the earliest days of the war and offered one of the few avenues of escape. She flew with the Army, Navy and Air Force in the UK and with forces in Asia, Australia and New Zealand, Canada and Africa, taking in her stride tasks from trainer to air ambulance and even prisoner evacuation.

The United States Army Air Force trained pilots on Tiger Moths borrowed from the RAAF and as the PT24, the DH82C Tiger Moth was ordered from DH Canada for home based US forces, but the aircraft were never delivered, diverted instead to the care of the RCAF.

Policy inspired colour changes had regularly occurred in all centres of military operation with the exception of Canada where Tiger Moths were exclusively yellow and black from first to last delivery. On July 5th 1940, King George VI authorised the substitution of the RCAF's roundel centre dot with a red maple leaf, but even this was not generally effected until January 1946 by which time the Tigers had moved on.

Immediately after the war RAF Tiger Moths resumed work in all yellow coats until military trainer schemes in the UK, Australia and New Zealand were standardised. But before long the type was finally declared obsolete, and discharged with honour.

It is gratifying that current owners wish to fly their aeroplanes in the colours carried whilst engaged in original employment, but attempting to accurately paint an aeroplane to conform to the unique style associated with a particular unit and period of history can be fraught with danger.

Luckily, archives held by the manufacturer, by museums, test establishments and historians can often identify basic colouring, so it is to be regretted that technically sound restorations continue to be spoiled by application of grossly inaccurate paint schemes.

Photographs of Tiger Moth R-5130 were extensively used for promotional purposes by de Havillands in the early period of the war. This pleasing July 1940 shot identifies some of the features of early militarised DH82A Tiger Moths which were subsequently changed in the light of intensive Service experience: underwing flare holders deleted and aileron mass balance weights removed; aileron control boxes realigned; straight pitot head replaced with a kinked variety; the yellow interplane struts were repainted dark green and the DH emblem discontinued.

Note the signal lamp which was wired to a Morse tapper in the cockpit. Material and Release specifications can be seen stencilled on the fabric near the tips of the lower mainplanes, ailerons, tailplane and elevators. The rear fuselage fabric is bootlaced along both lower longerons, providing immediate access for a thorough inspection of the rear pylon. R-5130 survived the war and was converted to a four seat Jackaroo by Rollason Aircraft in 1960, but she was written off in a crash in July 1961.

Groundcrew needed to be educated in the ways of the Tiger Moth and her Gipsy Major engine too. These RAFVR recruits are paying attention to a civilian instructor at Hatfield in January 1941. The boots, gaiters, gasmasks and haircuts are all courtesy of their new employer.
The camouflage of the second aircraft in the line has not yet been extended to the lower longeron, and the confluence of yellow, brown and green is nothing but a smudge in preparation perhaps, for an imminent visit to the dope shop.

Apart from the magnetos, the total electrical system of the military Tiger Moth was installed against the requirement to carry an assortment of stores and night flying equipment. Switchboards were fitted in the rear cockpits to control Morse tappers, navigation lights, panel illumination and underwing pyrotechnics.
Crouching beneath their greatcoats with collars set against the January weather which had already caused a sprinkling of snow, the boys in blue attend to the port flare holders whilst the instructor twiddles with the switches.

Tiger Moths built in Australia and New Zealand carried a number of locally developed modifications which were not only functional and convenient but provided an extra layer of safety and protection. Yet few if any of these Antipodean ideas were officially incorporated by the vast training assemblage in the UK where possibly the sheer volume of any retrospective upgrade programme rendered it impractical.

Whilst the UK training schools were still involved with the potentially lethal night flying flares, the New Zealanders developed an electric landing light system which could be folded back against the undersurface of the wing when not required.

Getting off under the hood!
Keeping straight on the very minimum of gyro controlled instrumentation in the rear cockpit, the instructor is borne aloft by his pupil in N-9181, "56" of No 10 EFTS at Yatesbury, Wiltshire.
Many of the aircraft at Yatesbury had, until just before this shot was taken in April 1940, worn the purple and yellow colours adopted by the Bristol Aeroplane Company's Reserve School, but soon all were camouflaged, even before total loss of their civilian identities. In September 1940 the whole EFTS was packed and shipped to its relocated base: the plains of India.

January 1941, and a trainee RAF pilot guides his Tiger Moth in to land, head inclined to the left, whilst his instructor maintains interest in the position of the horizon relative to his windscreen. Another crew holds off, ready to offer silent criticism.

N-9374 is fitted with aileron mass balances and flare holders, gas patch at the rear fuselage. and has a pennant attached to the starboard rear interplane strut. The paintscheme is a non-reflective matt finish, the most difficult for the ground crews to keep clean. Unusually, the fuselage serial number is located across the confluence of camouflage and yellow.

Learning to fly on a Tiger Moth in a British winter under the austerity of wartime conditions was for many, not one of the greatest pleasures of life. But whether the trainee pilots and instructors who were posted to Southern Rhodesia fully acclimatised to their hot, dusty surroundings is one of the great secrets of the war. In exchange for seasons of mist and mellow fruitfulness, the training machine was asked to cope with tolerably harsh operating conditions in which the physical state of the aeroplane structure and its performance were tested to the limits.

Morris built Tiger Moth T-8114 joined others from England and Australia at one of the five schools established by the Rhodesian Air Training Group after May 1940. This photograph was taken in 1942 and shows an all yellow Tiger Moth getting on with the job under a hot sun.

The Royal Navy claims to be the last UK Service user of the Tiger Moth, having purchased a batch of refurbished aircraft in 1956 for operation as glider tugs and Air Experience machines. They appeared at many aviation events and were readily distinguishable by their intricate pattern of vivid orange stick-on patches which had become a feature of training and transport aircraft of that era.

As part of its Historic Aircraft Flight based at Yeovilton in Somerset, the Royal Navy commissioned Tiger Moth T-8191, and along with stablemates Swordfish, Sea Fury, Firefly and occasional vintage jet, the Tiger Moth spends many UK summer weekends roaming the air display circuits.

In 1979 T-8191 by now painted in naval sea grey camouflage, was flown as the Royal Navy entry in the Famous Grouse Moth Rally from Hatfield to Perth in Scotland, but lost heavily in the fuel consumption element of the competition due to her excessive weight. Naval Regulations insisted that the crew should wear immersion suits and parachutes.

Jeremy Johnston took this British built Tiger Moth with him when he emigrated to Canada, where he fitted a modified fuel system which permitted sustained inverted flight. The aircraft became a familiar sight over Vancouver before a more slippery biplane took Jeremy's interest. The DH82A was sold to a former Tiger Moth owner in New York who flew the aeroplane back across the Rockie Mountains on a delivery trip lasting 36 flying hours. 270 gallons of fuel and almost 80 pints of oil were consumed.
In 1947 this aircraft (NL-775) was with Station Flight RAF Church Fenton, painted silver with a black top decking and No 19 Squadron blue and white chequerboard markings flanking the roundel. The aircraft was operated by the squadron as their aerobatic hack, and when sold out of the Service and acquired by Jeremy Johnston, he retained the chequers with the squadron's permission, but changed the silver to yellow for greater visual effect.

The underside dope scheme of a Tiger Moth whose colours are intended to represent any particular historical time slot is as important as that applied to the upper surfaces. Changes in the official camouflage schemes determined whether serial numbers were or were not carried under the lower mainplanes. When numbers were applied, their layout, size and style hardly changed although the type of roundel did.

The intention is that the serial number can be read both when the aircraft is heading towards the observer (starboard lower) and away from him (port lower).

Until 1936, all RAF trainer aircraft were painted in the standard colour of the day: "aluminium". Vertical red, white and blue rudder stripes had been carried until the autumn of 1934, but it is unlikely that any Tiger Moth Mk II would have worn them as their delivery schedule commenced in November. Thus, the RAF's newest trainers were painted an austere silvery grey brightened only by the uncomplicated roundels on wings and fuselage, with the serial number stencilled near the tailplane and repeated on the rudder.

In July 1936 the Air Ministry decreed that all trainer aircraft should be painted yellow with position, style and colour of the national markings remaining as before. Some units, preferring natural metal cowlings, had them buffed to perfection by enthusiastic groundcrews.

Camouflage gradually displaced yellow from the top surfaces of wings, fuselage and empennage from September 1938 although the colour was retained on all undersurfaces throughout the war. In August 1946, camouflage was completely removed and Tiger Moths were repainted 'Trainer Yellow' although officially there never was such a colour specification.

Reserve Command Tiger Moths represented by Ted Lay's faithful restoration in 1985, displayed their yellow wings, an eminently suitable colour for a neat biplane, for exactly four years before directives issued in 1950 placed all RAF, RAAF and RNZAF trainer aircraft back into the silvery grey situation, embellished only by broad yellow stripes around the rear fuselage and across the 'visual' surfaces of the mainplanes.

Between May 1941 and October 1943, No 19 EFTS, Royal Canadian Air Force, was stationed at Vinden in Manitoba. After a heavy snowfall, the Tiger Moths were quickly converted onto a ski undercarriage and flying continued with little or no interruption.

The worst weather problem experienced at Vinden was severe wind and the groundcrews were often required to attend to aircraft airborne at their pickets. It was usual, even in wartime Canada, for the majority of groundcrews to be civilians and therefore, not subject to military codes and discipline.

"4057", Gipsy Major powered DH82C, airborne from No 6 EFTS at Prince Albert, Saskatchewan, to which the aircraft had been posted in June 1940.

The skis were maintained in the neutral position by simple bungee cords, and rotated to their ground incidence as the aircraft touched down. When main undercarriage skis were fitted it was more usual for a steerable mini-ski to replace the tailwheel.

The DH82 Queen Bee was intended as a cheap and expendable pilotless target for anti-aircraft practise. Flown under the command of wireless apparatus situated in what would have been the trainee's cockpit, the front position was fitted with instruments and conventional controls which permitted the aeroplane to be flown between sites by a ferry pilot.

Apart from a wooden fuselage of the type built for the DH60GIII Moth Major, the Queen Bee incorporated Tiger Moth component parts for mainplanes, empennage, centre section and conventional undercarriage when floats were not fitted. The fuel tank was increased in size from the Tiger Moth's 19 gallons to 25 gallons, and powerplant was the standard Gipsy Major engine. The all up weight was quoted to be the same as the conventional Tiger Moth at 1,825 lb.

Based at units around the coast of Great Britain, in Malta, Gibraltar and Singapore, and aboard ships of the Royal Navy, the Queen Bees were flown under wireless control whilst gunners attempted to shoot them down. If the exercise was unsuccessful, the aircraft would be brought back to base, flown onto the water, serviced and sent off on a further mission. This photograph was taken during a Queen Bee launch from a ship of the Royal Navy on October 17th 1936, but not released for publication until January 1940, at which time the censor requested that the fuselage and rudder serial numbers should be deleted. In this print they were not.

As an alternative to the catapult launch, Queen Bees could be taken off from water whilst under wireless control.

In this 1937 action photograph, DH82 Queen Bee K-5107 is in the charge of No 3 Anti-aircraft Co-operation Unit based in Malta, and is seen during a fast run across the Mediterranean, probably under guidance from the fortress in the background.

Although frequently referred to as the DH82B, de Havillands never officially issued a 'B' type designation. The company nomenclature was simply DH82 Queen Bee.

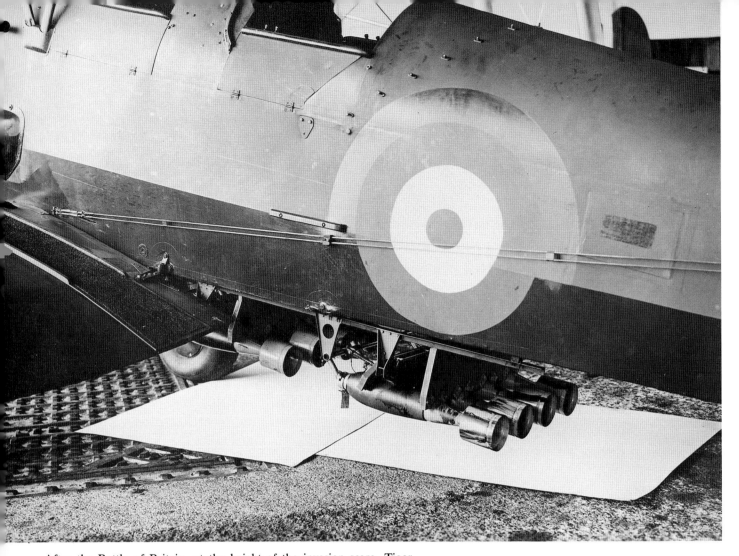

After the Battle of Britain, at the height of the invasion scare, Tiger Moths were fitted with bomb racks capable of carrying eight twenty pound bombs.

In its new configuration the Tiger Moth was subjected to 'Handling, Diving and Spinning Trials' at the Aeroplane and Armament Experimental Establishment, Boscombe Down, in October 1940, and the Report concluded: 'The aeroplane behaves in a satisfactory manner'. Tests included diving manoeuvres with a full complement of bombs attached. The test pilot reported that at throttle openings of more than a third he was limited by maximum permitted engine rpm, and in a dive of between 50 and 55 degrees he reached speeds up to 170 mph. It was recorded that all controls were satisfactory and no trouble was experienced during recovery.

Bomb-dropping tests were completed in level flight, in a prolonged dive at 170 mph and in a dive following a half roll, when the bombs fell away without fouling the undercarriage. Release was by pilot operated cable controlled from the rear seat.

Early in 1941 when invasion seemed less likely, the bomb racks and rails were removed, but their brief appearance had caused a flurry of excitement in some of the training schools where spin characteristics were believed to have been influenced by them. The result was a further series of tests at Boscombe Down and Farnborough in 1941 and a recommendation that led to Modification 112 – anti-spinning strakes.

Papers presented by test establishments covering the spinning nature of the Tiger Moth could be traced back to initial trials in 1931, since when it was recognised that the basic machine had considerably changed, particularly with regard to weight and distribution of load. Although aileron mass balance horns were later recommended for removal, bomb racks fitted under the front fuselage caused a disturbed airflow over the tail surfaces, a situation which called for aerodynamic refinement. The manufacturer offered Air Ministry Modification 112, a pair of light alloy pressings which were screwed onto the rear decking.

These photographs of Tiger Moth R-5082 were taken at Hatfield on December 27th 1941. The aircraft was one of a small initial batch fitted with Mod. 112 under the direction of the Ministry of Aircraft Production. From September 1942 all aircraft were modified prior to delivery and a retro-fit programme was initiated from December to cover aircraft in the field.

A proposed Tiger Moth Mk III did not proceed beyond one Mk II test vehicle, but the design studies showed a fin and rudder of outrageous proportions in addition to a new ventral fin and retention of the strakes.

Casualty evacuation from remote areas has always occupied a significant part of military thinking, and along with many other unlikely aeroplanes, the Tiger Moth has been modified in its time, as an air ambulance.

Following early experiments when space was made for a stretcher inside the rear decking, the RAAF refined their requirements in the light of practical experience, and converted a number of Tiger Moths to air ambulances at Laverton. RAAF Tiger Moth A17-543 was photographed in 1944 after completion of the casualty compartment and revised pilot's cockpit.

Sold into the civil market in 1948, A17-543 became VH-BIW with Connellan Airways at Alice Springs, serving the local community as an air ambulance. In 1964 the aircraft was re-registered VH-DYI and later became part of the Ken Orrman Collection by which time the airframe had reverted to standard configuration.

One of the problems with aeroplane restoration is the fact that airworthiness requirements may have been changed since the aircraft was certificated, and original profiles cannot be met.

To most outward appearances this Tiger Moth could be flying in dangerous skies between January 1941 and May 1942. However, the anti-spin strakes would not have been fitted until September 1942 at the earliest, by which time the fuselage roundels had been changed.

To maintain a Tiger Moth in the aerobatic category in UK skies, anti-spin strakes must be fitted. The decision was imposed by the authorities forty years after the final and definitive trials and aroused considerable controversy. When choosing a military colour scheme, the UK owner now has to consider the aerobatic option if the aeroplane is to be truly representative of that thin slot in history.

Tiger Moths operated by the wartime Indian Government were mostly issued with civil registration letters rather than military serials. The aircraft originated in Australia and the UK, and many survived to continue their dedicated routine of circuits and bumps with a post-war generation of trainees.

This photograph taken in May 1943, shows Indian Air Force officer cadets parading in front of their British built, civil registered Tiger Moths, awaiting inspection by Air Marshal Sir J. E. A. Baldwin, Deputy AOC in C, India.

Although there is no record of Tiger Moths being supplied directly to the Indian Air Force before the war, in March 1940 five IAF DH82A Tiger Moths were presented to the press at the Risalpur Training School. It is most probable that these aircraft were ex No 27 Squadron RAF, for the unit had been based in India with Tiger Moths and Hawker Harts from September 25th 1939. The K letter of the serial numbers was applied erroneously when the aircraft were taken on charge by the Indian Air Force, which fact led to much historical confusion.

The Indian authorities were keen to impress upon 1939's correspondents that via a rapid expansion scheme, scores of volunteers from both ethnic races would be selected and trained to the highest standards enjoyed by the Royal Air Force.

Between January 1940 and March 1946, the Royal Australian Air Force maintained 12 Tiger Moth equipped EFTSs spread throughout Australia. No 10 EFTS based at Temora, NSW, was the last to close, on March 12th 1946, and was at the height of its capacity during the southern winter of 1944 when this photograph was taken.

Tiger Moths of the RNZAF Central Flying School were identified as such by red rudders and engine cowlings in an otherwise all yellow colour scheme. Serial numbers were carried on the rudder in addition to the rear fuselage.

This photograph, taken at CFS Tauranga in 1943 or 1944, shows the school's Harvards in camouflage, silver, or silver with red appendages. The line of Oxfords reflects the same mixture.

Both Tiger Moths nearest the camera went on to civil careers, one becoming a club aircraft at Nelson in 1949 and the other a crop-sprayer in 1955.

In 1942, this Tiger Moth was on a low level sortie at 200 feet when the weather closed in unexpectedly and the pilot was forced to climb in cloud in order to cross high ground.

Whilst enveloped in the murk the propeller struck and burst a barrage balloon; the hot exhaust caused the balloon's hydrogen gas to ignite, setting the starboard side of the aircraft on fire.

The pilot immediately put the Tiger Moth into a port sideslip, and the flames were extinguished, but not before they had caused extensive damage to the fabric.

The aeroplane continued to base (believed to be Fairoaks) and landed safely having suffered no structural damage apart from the loss of her uniform.

In 1934, as part of the Rhodesian Territorial Army, an Air Wing was established using civil aircraft, although six Hawker Harts were transferred from the RAF in 1937.

The Southern Rhodesia Air Unit purchased a Tiger Moth in February 1938 which was used for instrument training and night flying. On the outbreak of war, the SRAU was reorganised with RAF assistance and became the Rhodesian Air Training Group.

RATG's first EFTS was established in May 1940 at Belvedere near Salisbury. Locally impressed aircraft were issued with SR serial numbers, but the majority of aeroplanes employed were Tiger Moths delivered from England or Australia which retained serial numbers allocated on production. They were painted yellow overall and remained so for the duration.

To release elements of the RAF Regiment whose duties included guarding air force aircraft and installations, an Air Askari Corps was organised which raised regiments from within the famous force. Under European officers, some NCOs and all troops were recruited from southern central African states.

Tiger Moth R-4916 under guard 'somewhere in Africa' retains a DH trademark on the outer face of the port rear interplane strut.

In 1939, Hugh Buckingham had been dispatched to New Zealand by DH to establish a factory in Wellington, and on December 22nd he flew the first Tiger Moth to come off the line: NZ740 had been assembled from parts shipped from Hatfield, and the historic test flight lasted a bare twenty five minutes.

An identical routine on April 30th 1940 was sufficient to pass out N-9249, one of the initial batch of diverted RAF aircraft, assembled from a British built kit. By the end of that year 165 Tiger Moths were on strength with the RNZAF. In December 1941, twenty Australian built aircraft arrived which swelled the inventory to 221, although the peak was not reached until a year later at 236 aircraft.

This photograph was taken at No 3 EFTS Harewood near Christchurch which was operational between August 1940 and July 1945. The all yellow Tiger Moths were never fitted with anti-spin strakes, neither did they carry bomb racks, and the type continued in uninterrupted service with the RNZAF as an elementary trainer until 1956. In line with RAF policy, in 1950 the colour scheme was changed to silver overall with yellow bands across the wings and around the rear fuselage.

The Air Training Corps was a valuable source of potential aircrew in the Commonwealth, and senior cadets, who were civilians, were permitted to fly in Service aircraft in wartime, although not during operations.

In New Zealand, due to the relatively remote nature of some centres of population, the RNZAF established an Air Training Corps Touring Flight based at Milson aerodrome, Palmerston North. The Flight operated up to five Tiger Moths which between May 1943 and VJ Day, toured the country offering air experience.

This view of an unidentified Tiger Moth clearly shows no serial number under the lower mainplanes, the ATC wings badge painted under the front cockpit door, the British type strapless oil tank and the local modification of what appears to be a centre section mirror.

Proving that open cockpit aviating in a warm climate can still be comfortable, the cadet disembarking from the rear cockpit is in short sleeved, open necked shirt and shorts, plus mandatory parachute. The flights were commanded from the front seat to allow the cadets the same feel of the aircraft which would be experienced under training.

No 8 EFTS was established by the Royal Australian Air Force at Narrandera, NSW on September 19th 1940 at an aerodrome construction cost of £79,000.

During the afternoon of December 6th, a freak storm swept across the field, following the line of the Murrumbidgee River. The aerodrome was fully active and the aircraft suffered accordingly: tie downs were ripped out of the ground, a taxying aircraft was thrown into the air and landed inverted, and an airman attempting to hold down a wingtip found himself thirty feet off the ground. Aeroplane damage was so severe that wings were simply chopped off the bent fuselages and piles of components were stacked by the main gate to await collection by the local Salvage Unit.

Before transport could be arranged, a new intake of cadet pilots arrived, to whom it was explained that the carnage was due to the antics of their predecessors. When the truth was finally revealed it was confirmed that few Tiger Moths suffered major damage as the direct result of training accidents, a credit to instructors and aeroplanes alike.

With the exception of the missing hyphen in the fuselage serial number, and gloss finish, Tiger Moth N-6985 sports what is otherwise an authentic camouflage scheme. The white bladed propeller would lose marks in a concours event, although having flown through a hedge since this photograph was taken in 1985, that matter will have resolved itself. Hundreds of Army glider pilots learned to fly on Tiger Moths before transferring to the wonders of motorless flight. Today, Army glider pilots fly only for sport, but it is not unknown for a Tiger Moth or a younger cousin to tow them to launch height behind the magical muscle of a Gipsy Major engine.

A long-term resident at Compton Abbas in Dorset, G-AHMN (N6985) was presented on permanent loan to the Museum of Army Flying at Middle Wallop in 1984.

In January 1941, Tiger Moths which had operated until then with camouflage terminating halfway down each fuselage side, were repainted with the colours extended to the bottom longerons. At the same time the dual A and B Scheme was discontinued in favour of a universal A Scheme. Under this system all "even" serial numbered aeroplanes had been painted in the A Scheme, whilst a mirror image, the B Scheme, was applied to all "odd" serialled aircraft.

From January 1941, tailplane and elevator upper surfaces and the fin and rudder were camouflaged; all under surfaces remaining yellow. The roundel on the fuselage sides was changed to Type A1, in which the red centre dot was surrounded by equal width banks of white, blue and yellow. The fin stripes of equal thickness red, white and blue were unchanged.

From May 1942 the fuselage roundel became Type C1 in which the yellow and white bands were of equal narrow width, and the red and blue wider at six inches. The fin flash was changed to incorporate just a two inch white vertical stripe between red and blue. These national marks remained the definitive scheme until August 1946 when camouflage was removed.

It is correct for DE-208 to be wearing a darker shade of earth brown on the upper mainplanes when compared with the lower, but the clear varnished interplane struts are non-standard and identify her as a post-war restoration.

For much of his working life, Ted Baker was an instructor with the London Transport Flying Club at Fairoaks aerodrome in Surrey. When it was decided to retire the Tiger Moth fleet in preference for something faster if not better, Ted's son David bought G-AIIZ, painted her in a 1941 camouflage scheme and had her delivered by CL44 to Hong Kong. The Tiger Moth aroused a deal of interest in the colony, and this pleasing shot was taken on November 25th 1981 during one of her many airborne tours of the waterfront.

The final coat of colours worn by Tiger Moths in Commonwealth service was adopted from August 1950 when the all over yellow was replaced by aluminium, with yellow bands on wings and rear fuselage.

For some aircraft, this was the third complete change of colours in only six years, evidenced by the build up of dope. When removing fairings during civilianisation earlier colours could be found underneath, confirming that the aircraft had not been dismantled when resprayed.

This photograph could have been taken on a sunny working day in the Fifties, but the tailwheel is strictly non-standard, and the only clue to the recent date of this non-military photographic sortie.

No 28 EFTS was opened at Mount Hampden, Salisbury, Rhodesia in April 1941. In May the following year, two Tiger Moths collided during the last stages of the approach and arrived on the ground locked together in an inverted position.

Twelve months later, to the day, May 14th 1943, an identical accident occurred in the same place, with precisely the same results, although on this occasion one pupil pilot was killed.

Such incidents were rare, given the thousands of landings each day at main base and satellite airfields, when dozens of aircraft would regulate themselves in terms of vertical and lateral separation with little assistance other than from the Mk 1 Eyeball.

The Tiger Moths based at Mount Hampden reflected another variation on the standard colour scheme by adopting a ring of red and white chequers around the rear fuselage, between the roundel and the tailplane. The reason was simply one of pride and nostalgia, for the senior engineering officer with 28 EFTS had previously enjoyed a posting with No 56 Fighter Squadron whose colours these were, and he adopted the markings for his new and less aggressive charges. And a closer look will reveal that between May 1942 and May 1943, other markings had changed too.

High over the Canadian prairies, a yellow and black DH82C Tiger Moth displays some of her locally evolved differences: footwells for the rear occupant's heels, mass balanced and tabbed elevators, raked undercarriage and heavy duty tailwheel.

Tiger Moth 4197 was taken on charge by the RCAF in September 1940 and allocated to No 15 EFTS at Edmonton from December. She was badly damaged in May 1942 and scrapped the following year.

At the height of the Battle of the Atlantic in 1941, de Havilland Canada became concerned that the flow of Gipsy Major engines which were manufactured in England, might be curtailed, a situation which would prove embarrassing as far as production and repair schedules were concerned.

The nearest most suitable and readily available engine was the American Menasco Pirate, delivering twenty horsepower less for an increase in weight, but it was an immediate solution to the incipient problem, and 136 airframes were built around the Pirate, which for all the world looked remarkably like a Gipsy Major.

Because the Pirate was fitted with a generator, ten aircraft were selected as Wireless Trainers for the RCAF, and 4883 is one of these, delivered under a contract which was completed between March and July 1941. A batch of DH82C4s, as the Menasco Moth was known by the manufacturer, ordered by the USAAF under the designation PT24, was not taken up and the aircraft were diverted to the RCAF.

When a Tiger Moth goes over onto its back, then the extent and nature of the damage will be related to the initiation speed of the manoeuvre, and the skill of the groundcrew during recovery.

In the absence of a crane, two lengths of rope and some manpower, carefully directed, is probably all that is needed. Using the propeller boss as a pivot point the aircraft can often be returned to near normality with little more than a broken rudder, splintered propeller, dented fuel tank, and a sheepish grin.

In 1947, Oxford University Air Squadron was one of eleven similar units still dependent on the Tiger Moth for flying training. Immediately post-war, many of the undergraduate members were pilots with a high number of flying hours, re-establishing their education after the great interruption that had offered them a broad spectrum of opportunities in aviation.

Tiger Moth T-6026 'RUOD' of the Oxford Squadron, was built at Cowley and based at both Abingdon and Manor Road aerodromes near the university. She served with ten different units including OUAS twice, before civilian sale in April 1948.

From March 1947, 25 Tiger Moth equipped Reserve Flying Schools were established in the UK. Between 1950 and 1953 most converted to Chipmunks, but by May 1954 all but one had been disbanded. The last, No 1 RFS at Panshanger, lingered on until February 1955.

The purpose of the Schools was to enable Reserve pilots to retain proficiency; to maintain a pool of experienced crews that could be tapped should the need arise. In addittion, the Reserve Schools provided facilities for Air Training Corps cadets to learn to fly and qualify for civil licences.

No 9 RFS was established at Woodley aerodrome in 1947 and by May was fully operational with its all yellow Tiger Moths, instructing cadets from the local ATC Squadrons.

This photograph was taken at Woodley on May 9th 1947 and in a typical press caption the writer asks:

"Are these our ace pilots of tomorrow?"

Before they followed the lead of the Reserve Schools and converted to Chipmunks, the University Air Squadrons were substantial users of Tiger Moths: Oxford, Cambridge, Birmingham, Durham, London, Nottingham, Southampton, Aberdeen, Edinburgh, Glasgow, Belfast, St. Andrews, Liverpool, Manchester and Leeds.

The RAF's Elementary Flying Training Schools were still well stocked with Tiger Moths in the late Forties and in addition there were Station Flights, Grading, Air Navigation, Test Pilot, Glider Pilot, Beam Approach and Air Traffic Schools, Conversion, Display, Recruitment and Maintenance Units. It was possible to tell what belonged to whom through a complicated system of code letters carried on the fuselage, usually straddling the roundel, and with some exceptions, all Tiger Moths were painted in their last coat of warpaint: the universal silver dope described in official handouts as "aluminium".

On March 7th 1953 a Tiger Moth 21st birthday party was organised at
Panshanger. Why 1953 when the prototype DH82 flew in 1931 and the
first DH82A made an appearance in 1933 is not known.
At the end of a long and distinguished military career it seemed unfair and
unwarranted to treat the old retainer in such a way, and it is probable that
the observing schoolboy at the right of the photograph is thinking that way
too.

The British Army's Elementary Flying Training School based at the Army Air Corps Centre at Middle Wallop, Hampshire, was one of the last Service users of Tiger Moths.

Seen during the final days of devoted service, DE709 "X-BD" flies over one of the most famous landmarks in England, and the site of the first military camp where aeroplanes were included in official Army manoeuvres forty years before the uniformed Tiger Moth retired.

Against a typical Naval Air Station backdrop, in this case Lossiemouth, Tiger Moth XL717 displays military markings appropriate to the late Fifties: silver overall with applications of "dayglo" panels on the cowlings, around the fin and rear fuselage and chordwise on selected wing areas.

The pilot's leather helmet has changed to standard issue bone dome but the airframe is much the same including dented top cowl and oil tank, although the tail skid has been replaced with a composite device for the attachment of glider tow cables.

XL717 began life with the RAF in 1940 as a Morris built aircraft (T-7291). Following demobilisation she was added to the civil register in 1956 as G-AOXG but sold to the Royal Navy in May 1957. Upon retirement from the Navy who had elected to allocate a new serial number, XL717 was presented to the Fleet Air Museum at Yeovilton where she is maintained as a static exhibit.

Nobody is left in any doubt as to the ownership of T-8191. At the time this photograph was taken, T-8191 was painted silver with yellow trainer bands, but she is currently maintained in an airworthy state by the FAA Historic Aircraft Flight at Yeovilton, camouflaged in a naval grey/green scheme, one of the many she has worn since joining the Senior Service in October 1946.

5. Look what they've done

The Tiger Moth was designed to be a training aeroplane; a machine that was not difficult to fly, but one that was difficult to fly well. As such, she was a forgiving, robust aeroplane, sound in wind and limb.

In view of the sheer volume of her production, the vast quantities of airframe and engine spares that were manufactured to support her, and the rock bottom prices that these realised when ex-military hardware was released onto the civil market, there is little wonder that some operators tended to take liberties.

The spares backing for a worldful of Tiger Moths lasted fully twenty years after Service release before shortages were reported in some quarters. In the UK, a Fifties import ban on foreign light aeroplanes did little to stir imaginative home creations although there were some, using Tiger Moth components! Instead, organisations and owners worked their way through stocks of still cheap government surplus and where necessity can always be relied upon as the mother of invention, so Tiger Moths were readily adapted to the needs of the hour.

Ingenious modifications were invented to help turn the old open cockpit basic trainer into a comfortable touring aeroplane, else a realistically competitive aerobatic mount. Tiger Moths were disguised out of all recognition for starring roles in big screen epics whilst others, naked behind little but an unfamiliar shade of

Look what they've done! A. J. Whittemore (Aeradio) at Croydon Airport was only one of several companies who bid for government surplus Tiger Moths. Most of the aircraft were flown from their disposal units, but some were carried by surface, carefully dismantled and loaded onto purpose-modified lorries, themselves military castaways. Upon collection, the Service markings were crudely obliterated and civil letters applied in an equally undignified manner.
The Tiger Moth on the lorry, pictured early in 1954 at Croydon, was about to join thirty of her cousins stacked against the walls of the hangar behind a quartet of ex-RAF Proctors. By the following August, N-6919 had flown again, prior to joining a growing fleet of civil Tiger Moths on glider tugging duties in France.

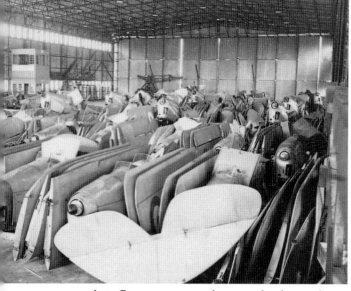

From across Africa in 1946, Tiger Moths arrived in small groups at No 3 Air Depot in Cape Town. Here, they were dismantled, packed into purpose-built crates and shipped to India where, during the next five or six years, they appeared on the civil register.

At a time when ex-Service Tiger Moths were realising £50 each, crates alone must have been worth more than the aeroplanes.

greasepaint, flew as supporting cast in the orchestrated armadas, most often on the side of the baddies. One Tiger Moth, tailored to the needs of the American motion picture industry was spectacularly crashed, rebuilt, and crashed again on a different assignment. No doubt she has survived to dive again.

Tiger Moths have lived with added systems (there were precious few to take away), with upper or lower wings removed, an assortment of locally applied brakes and tailwheels, windscreens and canopies, skis and floats. She has been flown with a single cockpit or with four seats, as an agricultural spreader or executive taxi. Made from wood and equipped with rudimentary wireless, earlier cousins had been catapulted into the air with the prime aim of being shot out of it again.

But the silly season eventually passed, and the survivors largely have been returned to their original build specifications, retaining a miniature wireless perhaps as a concession to crowded airspace, or tailwheel and taxibrakes for practical application when restricted to operations from paved runways.

Paint schemes have passed from almost universal silver, through bizarre and tasteless concoctions of colour, to civil and more particularly military patterns which current owners believe to reflect past glories, when the Tiger Moth was engaged upon her primary task.

PG685 was a May 1944 product of Morris Motors but spent most of her war in storage pending disposal. On August 1st 1946 she was delivered to the Royal Netherlands Air Force as A4. Until March 1955, A4 was based at Woensdrecht Air Force Base before transfer to 323 Squadron at Leeuwarden in May, where this photograph probably was taken. Note the "bone domes" awaiting collection from near the port interplane struts and fin, just as soon as the crew have been settled in. Processed through the Aircraft Material Depot at Gilze-Rijen in November 1960, A4 was allocated to the New Guinea Air Defence Command from August the following year in a new capacity of glider tug. She was joined by A29 and both aircraft were donated to the Kroonduif company's flying club when the Dutch withdrew from the territory late in 1962.
The two aircraft eventually found their way to the USA where A4 became N5444, but documented against a spurious builder's number which might lead historians to believe she had arrived from South America!

Opposite: This scene was as typical as any in the Croydon hangars during the early Fifties: dust-laden components from a number of differing aircraft types vie with stacked Tiger Moth fuselages for peripheral hangar space. The Tigers show varying degrees of cannibalisation ranging from fuel tanks to empennage to anti-spin strakes, to navigation lights to windscreens; all the first aid kits have been removed from their boxes. There are two styles of fin stripes, one fuselage has no trainer bands, another has square doors and a serial which identifies it as an impressed pre-war aircraft. Most interesting perhaps is the sliding canopy arrangement fitted to N-6808.
All five of these aircraft were converted to full civilian status: three were exported to Germany, one to Belgium and the last to New Zealand.

The earliest batches of Tiger Moths sold to the post-war French Government for civilian use were supplied from store, when deletion of the RAF marks and application of registration letters was the near total conversion factor. The camouflage dope scheme was straight Morris Motors' issue.

As the aircraft were engaged in glider tugging duties, the tailskid was adapted locally to accept a towhook. Modifications to the rudder, considered necessary for clearance of the tow-rope, left the rear end of the aeroplane looking stark and incomplete.

Tiger Moths supplied under additional French governmental contracts left the UK during the early Fifties having been subjected to thorough overhaul, mostly at Croydon. All 200 aeroplanes supplied were eventually doped silver with black registration letters.

The recipient aero clubs operated the Tiger Moths under official sponsorship and were forbidden to sell them, but were permitted to swap aeroplanes and parts amongst themselves. At the termination of the subsidies after twenty years, the 60 surviving aircraft were sold off for what could be raised, the highest prices seemingly being governed by the proximity of the vendor to the Channel coast.

In Australia and New Zealand where the business of sowing seed or spreading nutrients or pesticides from aircraft over thousands of acres, was developing into a necessity rather than a luxury, the agricultural aviators developed an insatiable desire for cheap, adaptable aircraft. The Tiger Moth was their answer. Examples were advertised in the UK, completely rebuilt, crated and ready for shipment at £1,100 per pair.

This sorry sight was photographed at Tamworth, NSW, on October 8th 1964. Inappropriately registered VH-BUM, the Tiger Moth had once been the proud A17-376 of the Royal Australian Air Force. Converted to carry a hopper where once the patient instructor had sat, the aircraft was stripped of the rear fabric and even the undercarriage fairings in an unrelenting endeavour to shed weight. Note the crash pylon which was a late mandatory modification; the wrinkled state of the rudder trailing edge; yet the neat touch of the DH monogrammed wheel hub caps, protecting the bearings.

And at the end of the day, when the faithful Tiger had served her best, she was cast out to die. VH-ACJ was unceremoniously dumped after a crash in December 1964. She had previously been VH-AKQ, AYY, BYF and RVC, but always No. 120, a product of the Mascot works in 1940.

High wing Tiger: Tiger Moth fuel tank, centre section, basic fuselage, landing gear, nose cowling and top wings; tailplane, elevator, fin and rudder are very Moth Minorish; registration is appropriate.

This apparition was known as the TK7¼, and was a product of the de Havilland Aeronautical Technical School, some of whose delinquent members presented G-ASP to an astonished gathering at the Hatfield Open Day on June 26th 1953, where, not surprisingly, she failed to become airborne.

Low wing Tiger: it could be a two seat DH53 or a cross between that and a Miles Hawk, but it is a Tiger Moth with a cut down undercarriage and the top wings and centre section removed. The re-positioned interplane struts bind the structure together.

Before and during the First World War, French training schools first taught their pupils to taxi in similar airframes that were incapable of flight. Once the pupil was sufficiently competent at maintaining a straight line, he was introduced to a machine that could just be persuaded to hop.

This Tigerish device, named the Hoppity Trainer, was built from Tiger Moth components in Southern Rhodesia in 1943, and was allocated to the local Air Training Corps as a runabout.

A Tiger showing its stripes. You love it or you hate it, but either way it catches the eye.

Apart from anything else, the paint scheme produced to the requirements of owner Neil Cottee in Australia, highlights the talent of the spray artist. The tiger's head blends perfectly into an area of cowling and oil tank which causes endless contour problems on basic Tiger schemes.

Full marks to the photographer too, for he has picked a background which permits maximum subject impact.

France has always been an airminded nation and due to enthusiasts like Jean Salis who has collected almost anything that flies, at least part of the nation's aviation heritage has been salvaged.

From a cache of Tiger Moth parts declared surplus by the Air Force, Jean Salis has built several World War I replicas for exhibition or film and television work. Although the fuselage might be devoid of top decking, this replica Albatross C2 is little more than a thinly disguised DH82A.

Hannu Riihela, designer of high performance gliders, discovered during the rebuilding of Tiger Moth OH-ELA, that the derelict airframe was devoid of undercarriage legs, wheels, tailskid, instruments and cowlings, and more importantly, a Gipsy Major engine.

Ex-RAF Tiger Moth T-6958 had been sold to Finland in 1951 but was not repaired following an accident two years later. The wreck was kept in store until Hannu bought in it 1970.

The engine problem was resolved by designing and building a new front bulkhead and bearer arrangement and installing a 180 hp Lycoming 0-360, complete with starter, battery and generator. The undercarriage is original but fitted with wheels from a Beech Musketeer.

Registered in the Experimental class as OH-XLA, the Tiger Moth has not unnaturally been used for glider tugging, has operated on skis and in a floatplane. Rates of climb in excess of 1,500 feet per minute have been recorded.

Hannu Riihela sold the aeroplane to a group of pilots based in Helsinki known as the Finnish Tiger Moth Association. She has spent some time as a publicity vehicle, and in the early Eighties, celebrated Christmas suspended from the ceiling of a Helsinki departmental store whilst Santa Claus snoozed in the rear cockpit.

Take a Wackett and remove the canopy. Take a Tiger Moth and remove the windscreen, doors and the centre decking. Screw on a pair of guide rails, add the canopy, and you have a practical touring biplane, which can, after all that trouble, be flown with the canopy open.

Gipsy Moth coupés found little favour but the Tiger Moth has been canopied with greater success, although even the most efficient lidding systems have subsequently been removed in the quest for originality. In addition to her Wackett canopy, VH-BRM, still active in Victoria, carries a glider tow hook on the tailskid, a generator bolted to the undercarriage V strut, radio aerial on the rear fuselage, and apart from the astonishingly fierce dentistry, a carburettor intake filter on the starboard cowling. This external teardrop was a modification employed on all Australian built Tiger Moths following experience with UK supplied machines which carried a conventional ram air scoop, but no protection against the dustier environment of RAAF training bases.

Opposite: No show at the Royal Newcastle Aero Club's Maitland aerodrome would be complete unless the Red Baron and Sir Percy Goodfellow meet in a hectic duel. The fact that both sides in the conflict are apparently operating identical equipment is lost on the public; it is the colour schemes, the badges of identity, that are of greatest significance. But there are few who would advocate that the popularity of the old Tiger Moth could ever be enhanced by a reversal of her fighting colours.

A UK government embargo on the import of foreign light aircraft during the post-war era resulted in some clever carpentry which aimed to create silk purses from the proverbial sow's ears.

One of the earliest UK Tiger Moth coupé conversions was Bill Woodhams' Coventry-based G-AIZF, which apart from what appears to be a fixed extension behind the glasshouse, bears a remarkably neat and practical similarity with Australian Wackettisation.

Four "Super Tigers" were converted by Rollason Aircraft and Engines for the Tiger Club at Redhill between 1958 and 1960. The name of the first, G-APDZ "The Bishop", was in recognition of the outstanding contribution to Tiger Moth related activities by the Club's CFI, C.A. Nepean Bishop.

"Bish" as he was always known, had been the leading light in a pre-war group which owned a DH60 Moth at Woodley, and had published several articles covering ownership and operation of light aircraft. Bish was the ideal choice for "CFI" although the Tiger Club did not offer instruction, rather conversion onto the different types in the fleet.

"The Archbishop" was a natural follow-up and the third and fourth aircraft continued the ecclesiastical lineage with "The Deacon" and "The Canon". The Canon was slightly different from the previous three in that it had ply leading edges on all four wings, creating a more efficient section. All Tiger Moths built in Australia uniquely employed hard leading edges although this simple customisation was never accepted as standard elsewhere.

When the Tiger Club decided to convert standard Tiger Moths into "Super Tigers" the aim was to produce a competition aerobatic aircraft capable of giving the opposition a run for its money.

To achieve a clean airframe it was necessary above all else to make one major modification: fuel, normally situated in the centre section, was removed to the front cockpit where its plumbing system was suitably arranged in order to provide a full "inverted" supply. The gap left in the centre plane was carefully faired over. Other changes involved deleting walkways and anti-spin strakes; fairing in the front cockpit with a detachable lid, fitting a token windscreen at the rear cockpit and reprofiling the doors. A metal propeller was mated with the uprated Gipsy Major engine, and the area of the elevators was increased.

The Super Tigers performed well, and were perhaps, the last great advance in Tiger Technology. Shortly after their brief heyday, other more nimble types found their way into competition aerobatics, and the Tiger was at last outclassed.

But when the Super Tiger was required to carry a passenger, mods. to the mods. had to be invented. Faced with the lack of a front seat, a hammock was provided for the occupant who now displaced the fuel supply. There was no provision for a front windscreen so prolonged flight was blatteringly uncomfortable. Fuel was carried in a tank temporarily located at the centre section, mounted on a cradle welded from redundant cabane struts. The on/off cock was operated by ARB approved string which fed down into the rear cockpit: double string for fuel on, single strand for off. It might look crude but it was functional and practical and permitted the aeroplane to operate cross-country, with an engineer or necessary associate on board.

Old struts and string: every layman's analysis of the classical biplane.

In March 1957, at a time when the selling price of a completely rebuilt Tiger Moth was still a fraction of any post-war competition, serious studies were made in contemplation of the aeroplane as a modern tourer or air taxi. Glasshouses of varying degrees of efficiency were added to the Tiger's top decking, but the Rollason answer was to offer a low, streamlined half canopy, completely enclosing the passenger's front cockpit, but leaving the pilot's head in the air, much in the fashion of the European Fox Moth of 1932. In this photograph the pilot is wearing a leopard skin helmet!

The Tiger Taxi was a relatively fast machine and quiet too, with its extended exhaust pipe. Unusual was the undercarriage mounted generator, with the almost mandatory glider tow hook offering some flexibility in tasking.

G-AOXS is pictured in flight over Baginton aerodrome, Coventry, scene for many years of the National and King's Cup Air Races. The bold statement painted on the ramparts of the Sir W. G. Armstrong Whitworth Aircraft factory could have been equally appropriate to Rollason's spirit: Pioneers of Progress.

Opposite and below: In 1956, the Wiltshire School of Flying based at Hampshire's Thruxton aerodrome, embarked on a design study for a high wing four seater aircraft built from Tiger Moth components. The idea was abandoned. Ten years later, the same school was investigating the possibility of a low wing machine, again built from Tiger Moth parts, and a mock-up was constructed at Thruxton but progressed no further, at which point the business was sold and the project slipped into oblivion.

In the meantime, Ronald Prizeman, a graduate of aeronautical engineering at Cranfield and a professional designer, was contracted by the school to develop a four seat touring and training aircraft from the basic Tiger Moth.

The project became reality on March 2nd 1957, when former Spitfire test pilot Geoffrey Shea-Simonds, flew the prototype. The aircraft was called the Thruxton Jackaroo and was offered in the four seat trainer/tourer version or as a bulk carrier with a single pilot's seat offset on the port side. Removal of the passenger cabin top and installation of a hopper was all that was necessary to accomplish the change in configuration.

To accommodate four people, the fuselage side frames of the standard Tiger Moth were moved further apart and new cross frames installed. A wider undercarriage track and fairings between the wings and centre section fuel tank were required, otherwise the rigging and mainplanes were not modified. The empennage was standard Tiger Moth too, but the fuselage was lengthened to provide baggage space behind the cabin, and a supplementary engine frame was fitted between the bulkhead and standard bearers which lengthened the nose by eight inches.

The tourer/sprayer quick conversion model was not taken up commercially and the prototype was finished as a standard cabin model but sold to Nigeria ironically as a sprayer. Owners were encouraged to fly their Tigers to Thruxton and after a ten day wait and payment of £600, fly them away as four seat Jackaroos. Twenty aeroplanes were completed at Thruxton plus nine others for a frustrated export order, but at least eight of these were reduced to spares to service the School's own fleet, which was rarely less than ten operational aircraft at any one time.

Ex-RAF Tiger Moths delivered to the Dutch RLS (Government Aviation School) and NLS (National Aviation School) were discovered to have a somewhat greater rudder movement than the single example which had operated in Holland pre-war.

The civil authorities were alarmed that the extra deflection might jeopardise the aircraft's suitability as a primary trainer, and newly delivered machines were not used in that role until agreed modifications had been installed.

Flight trials were conducted in September 1946 using an aircraft whose rudder movement was artificially restricted, and as a result, three alternative modification schemes were proposed. What became known as the "Fokker tail" was chosen and both RLS and NLS fleets of over 30 aircraft each were progressively fitted with the ugly appendages.

The "primary trainer" concern was expressed by the civil authorities alone, and none of the 67 aircraft

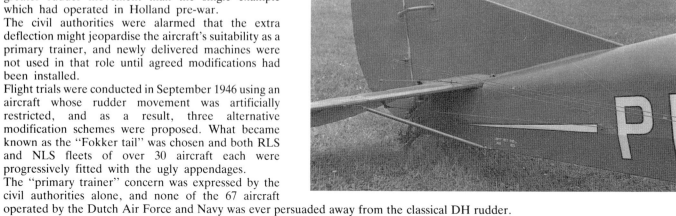

operated by the Dutch Air Force and Navy was ever persuaded away from the classical DH rudder. Once declared obsolete and released from duty, many of the modified Dutch aircraft were sold, notably to the USA, where they were reconverted. Meanwhile, private owners based in Holland who enjoyed some of the privileges of foreign passports, were not required to remove their elegant rudders, a concession only recently granted to Dutch nationals, presumably, on account of the changed status of the Tiger Moth.

Even after its closure, Croydon airport echoed to the beat of Gipsy Major engines. One of the very last Tiger Moths to leave the site was an ex-military airframe, T-7438, which was sold by the RAF in 1954 and converted in 1961 by Film Aviation Services for a starring role as a Fokker D VII in the magnificent film *Lawrence of Arabia*.

Two additional Tiger Moths were modified to represent Rumpler CVs for the same production; the tail ends of both machines were disguised by the simple addition of Fokker fins and rudders, but as the aircraft were seen only in long shot, nobody raised any objections.

This "Fokker D VII" photographed at Croydon was painted to represent an aircraft of the Turkish Forces during their Arabian campaign.

Prototype DH82A G-ACDA joined No 1 EFTS at Hatfield in 1933, resplendent in maroon and silver, the house colours of the de Havilland fleet.

In October 1940, in company with many others, G-ACDA donned her military coat and became BB724, continuing business as before. On July 8th 1942, BB724 was damaged in a landing accident at the Relief Landing Ground at Holwell Hyde, and after repair was not returned to Hatfield but joined the Royal Navy, serving at Eglinton for twenty days prior to return to the RAF at Kemble on August 19th 1943.

On September 13th, BB724 was sold to Bertram Arden, and stored on his farm near Exeter. How this military Tiger Moth was sold out of the service and into civilian hands during wartime, and before Tiger Moth production had ended, is unclear.

The camouflaged aircraft remained in store until the late Seventies, when she was removed, ironically to Kemble, for a major overhaul, during which time G-ACDA was repainted in her old civilian colours.

During a test flight in June 1979, only days prior to joining the Moth fleet at Hatfield, assembling for the Famous Grouse Rally, the engine stopped. Diving the aircraft in an abortive attempt to restart the motor by windmilling the propeller resulted only in serious loss of height and commitment to an immediate forced landing.

Side slipping round a tree and preparing to three point in what appeared to be a suitable field, the aircraft collided with a shrouded pylon, became entangled in high voltage wires and burst into flames. The two occupants used the starboard lower wing as a ladder, stepping to safety, but were forced to watch helplessly whilst the faithful old prototype disappeared in a cloud of smoke.

110

6. All in a day's work.

Since the first days when she was promoted as a trainer, the Tiger Moth has seen action in numerous alternative roles whilst retaining her modest profile. It has not always been necessary to substantially alter the airframe; the open cockpit biplane's basic configuration is as adaptable as any and more so than most. Flying men in search of innovation eyed their Tiger Moths with a confidence born of maturity before reaching for their slide rules (or their helmets and goggles more likely) to put their faith to practical test.

So the solid, dependable trainer became a workhorse: a crop-sprayer, glider tug, circus performer, aerobatic specialist, photographic mount, paradropper, tourer, seaplane, filmstar, recruiter, joyrider, racer, advertising gimmick, deck lander and museum exhibit. Nothing, it seems, was or indeed is, beyond the capabilities of the DH82; nothing that is, which might be considered to fall within the specification for an honest day's work.

In 1947 it was easy to buy a Tiger Moth with a full Certificate of Airworthiness for a few hundred pounds. Potential purchasers were offered almost any colour they required, as long as it was silver. Cooking Tigers, as they were known, were freely available.

Co-ownership groups and clubs were formed, and if formally constituted, qualified for a cash rebate against petrol costs under a government scheme which recognised the pilots as a national asset: they could be called upon in times of possible stress.

In August 1947, the ladies and gentlemen of the Midland Bank Flying Club presented themselves to the press. Some of the men might well have been ex-Service pilots; operational types or instructors; others may never have flown before joining the bank.

Judging by the state of the grass, the summer dresses and the rolled sleeves, the English summer of 1947 must have been exceptional. The Tiger Moth no doubt, put in maximum effort.

The member in the aeroplane is wearing a parachute. Most civil Tiger Moth operators built a plywood box that filled the pan of the bucket seats, originally designed to take a military parachute, then piled loose cushions onto that. The thought of abandoning a Tiger Moth in flight rarely occurred to any civil operator.

In December 1951, Gabrielle Patterson, a former ATA pilot of immense experience and skill, was engaged as Chief Flying Instructor with the Lancashire Aero Club at Barton. A lady flying instructor was so rare that the appointment made newspaper headlines.

Many of the larger clubs in the UK bid annually for contracts to train ATC cadets, and in some cases only the success of the application permitted the clubs to remain solvent.

It is something of a mystery that "Gabbie's" pupil, Sgt. Brian Taylor of 2183 Squadron, Air Training Corps, should have been training with the Lancashire Club at all, for in December 1951, Barton was host to No 2 Reserve Flying School. In January 1951, No 2 RFS had converted from Tiger Moths to Chipmunks, but in December of the same year they re-equipped again, with Tiger Moths!

A view as typical as any at a British aerodrome in the late Forties and early Fifties: an Auster and a trio of workstained Tiger Moths, some classic motor cars and a mobile fuel bowser.

Tiger Moth G-AHNX was registered to the Luton Flying Club in June 1946 and crashed at Luton in May 1948. Tiger Moth G-AINU, had crashed in Kent the previous week. The Club committee would have been displeased.

This placid scene; the windsock scarcely disturbed by the breeze, the expansive green acres of the airfield, the trees, hedges and country lanes of rural Bedfordshire; all were shortly to be obliterated under a sea of concrete as the package holiday business created vital opportunities for Luton International Airport.

Having never shaken off the public image of a barmy, barnstorming biplane, the Tiger Moth has been used to full effect by enthusiastic travelling circuses in exploiting that popular but misconceived reputation. In spite of becoming a vintage lady and prized possession, air circus Tiger Moths continue to be hurt whilst demonstrating their avowed intent to "make em laugh".

On the other hand, what a thrill to sit as front seat passenger when chopping the ribbon proclaiming "Happy Birthday".

Sure beats cutting a cake, Wilbur.

April 1959, and a new public house is commissioned at Rochester, Kent. Not the "Courage and Barclay", the "Rose and Crown" or the "Goat and Compasses", but "The Tiger Moth". What could have been a difficult and expensive logistical exercise in provisioning the occasion with a real Tiger Moth was actually very simple. The aeroplane was pushed through the main gate of Rochester airport, ruddered left, and a couple of hundred yards ahead was the Tiger Moth's car park. All very civilised. Unfortunately, exactly seven years later the aeroplane was written off, but we have it on the best authority that business at the "Tiger Moth" is doing very nicely.

In March 1966, the then biggest military transport aeroplane in the world, the USAF's C141A Starlifter, made its first visit to Canberra, Australia, touching down at RAAF Base Fairbairn. The Tiger Moth, owned jointly by a pilot and an engineering officer from No 34 Squadron RAAF, was chosen for this publicity shot to emphasise the bulk of the big jet.

"Have you seen a reindeer?"
Not much fun being Father Christmas, forced to fly an open cockpit Tiger Moth in the depths of the European winter. One senior air force officer, persuaded to impersonate the old fellow and exude seasonal goodwill, almost stuffed his Tiger Moth into the children's jelly when a set of flowing false whiskers obliterated his forward view at the critical moment. In this 1984 photograph, the flagship of the Tiger Club was caught during the evening's rounds steered by jolly old St. Nick, when everyone else in the country was turning up the central heating.

She started life as A17-565, the 1000th Tiger Moth to be assembled by de Havillands at Mascot. Not until June 1958 did the RAAF decide that A17-565 could be released, and she left Wagga Base to become a sprayer. Business was slow for in seven years she accumulated just 370 hours. For five more years she flew not at all, but instead received a fixed canopy. With such a lid in 1970 she arrived in the USA to become N17565; a subtle touch.

Ill health forced a quick sale, and the Tiger Moth was registered G-BCRD, sold to a British businessman living in Connecticut.

It was business that took the new owner Richard Dent, with his Moth, to Switzerland, where local markings were applied and a bold concept confirmed. Taking up a handsaw, Richard cut off the canopy leaving himself with no alternative but to complete the reconversion to open cockpits. Not unusually, the task took longer than anticipated but the momentous decision has never been regretted.

Opposite: One of over a hundred Tiger Moths based in the United States is N39DH owned by Kurt Hofschneider of Lancaster, New Jersey, who maintains N39DH in pristine condition and has applied a matt camouflage scheme, unusual in an age of high gloss. Concessions to the modern operating environment include brakes and steerable tailwheel.

The New York skyline is familiar to Kurt's Tiger Moth which has been involved in several vintage aircraft flypasts, and on one occasion was enrolled as an attack fighter when an inflatable King Kong created mock terror in the streets.

West Front by Henry Flitcroft, circa 1755.
Moth de Havilland, circa 1938.

In 1980 the de Havilland Moth Club was invited by Lord and Lady
Tavistock to rally in the grounds of Woburn Abbey, an estate well used to
the sight and sound of Gipsy engines, for Lord Tavistock's great
grandmother had owned several different Moths and flew from these very
acres.

The 1980 meeting was a success and return invitations have been issued
every year since, with the event growing bigger and more colourful, yet
retaining the special atmosphere created by informality and the sense of
history.

This magnificent study of a Tiger tug in action heightens all the senses. Feel the power! The Eagle glider, a heavy two-seater, is correctly positioned, the glider pilot maintaining the relativity of the tug's top wings.

Tiger Moths were once a common sight at any gliding club, but as operating costs increased and spares holdings diminished, the old workhorses were replaced by younger, more efficient cousins.

For several years after the end of the war, the Royal Air Force mounted annual exhibitions during Battle of Britain week.

The centrepiece of the London display on Horse Guards' Parade, was the recreation of a Fighter Command Control Room at the height of the battle; personnel would act out a typical raid plot to the accompaniment of sirens and the noise of explosions.

Horse Guards' Parade was liberally spread with aircraft of the period, ours and theirs, together with an injection of current equipment in an attempt to interest a new generation of military pilots.

Tiger Moth NL985 of the RAF Display Unit was on parade in the late sixties together with a Supermarine S6B and Gloster Gladiator, amongst others, picketed on the perimeter of the parade ground close by government buildings still suffering, at that time, from the effects of hundreds of years of London smog.

NL985 was also displayed during the Queen's Review of the Royal Air Force at Abingdon in 1968 after which the proud machine was placed in the semi-complete surroundings of the Royal Air Force Museum at Hendon. During a lapse in security, mindless guttersnipes set her alight; the Tiger Moth was completely destroyed, but attempts to burn other aircraft failed.

"Props into ploughshears".
Ralph Wefel, Founder and first President of the US Antique Airplane Association Moth Club, attempts to redress the balance during the spring of 1971. The Tiger Moth had landed at Happy Canyon Ranch near Santa Ynez in California. The field was short and soft with a downhill gradient, and a whipping 35 knot cross wind. It may be as well that the Tiger refused to budge for if she had, repairs to the pilot in addition to the tail, would surely have been inevitable!

When the controlling authorities in the Sudan realised that its annual crop of cotton could be protected by pesticides sprayed from the air and acre for acre, more cheaply than by any other method, fleets of agricultural aeroplanes and helicopters were contracted on a seasonal basis to work from Khartoum.

At Bembridge aerodrome on the Isle of Wight, a pair of Crop Culture Tigers have been prepared ready for shipment. The fuselage of G-ANRE is positioned alongside a makeshift ramp leading into the hold of a Bristol Freighter. The Tiger Moth's undercarriage has been removed, although the fuselage rests on a dolly constructed around a pair of Tiger Moth wheels. Two sets of wings are stacked awaiting loading. This photograph was taken from inside the maintenance hangar which explains why the lampshade at the right of the shot is not hanging from a cloud.

The attrition rate amongst agricultural machines was high. G-ANFK crashed in 1957 and was written off, and in September of the same year, G-ANRE met a similar fate whilst earning her keep in The Cameroons.

Tiger Moth preparing for work, April 1953.

Ten years after the peak of the wartime training programme, Tiger Moths were well established in their second careers. These were often short-lived, terminated by physical contact with mother earth or destroyed by the corrosive action of their cargo.

Support vehicles and employees trailed the spreaders around New Zealand and Australia, loading, preparing and reloading in the shortest possible time, for acreage covered meant earlier transfer to the next contract and bigger bonuses at the end of the day.

In September 1959, engine companies would have been excited about the prospects for Jet and Rocket Assisted Take Off, the de Havilland Engine Company included. But Tiger Moth G-ANCT is not rising on a stream of rocket exhaust, neither has the dependable Gipsy Major literally blown a gasket.

Armed with nothing more lethal than a battery of rotary atomisers, possibly an oil cooler, certainly a modified front cockpit and vast wrap-around windscreen, the aeroplane is demonstrating her spread and spray technology to a press gathering at Cranfield.

According to official lists, G-ANCT was an unconverted military hulk, scrapped at Christchurch in 1956, yet three years later she displayed a remarkable soundness of wind and limb in the hands of a Crop Culture demonstration pilot.

The conversion of Tiger Moth Trainer to Tiger Moth Farmer was not simply a matter of cutting a large hole in the bottom of the fuselage through which to dump the load at the tug of a string. The equipment fitted to the old stagers was more complex than any military system which had ever been previously demanded.

The dispensing methods varied with the task: main hopper distribution for phosphates and seed through a channel below the fuselage; liquids via spray bars attached to the under surface of the lower mainplanes, or atomisers bolted to the top.

Britten-Norman developed rotary atomisers for their own Crop Culture fleet of Tiger Moths, and marketed the gear during the late Fifties. The systems were energised by wind power: the four bladed fans were locked off or on at the discretion of the pilot via a simple Bowden cable.

Tiger Moth G-AMVF attacks potatoes in East Anglia. The pilot had to fly steadily and accurately on each pass to ensure maximum coverage at the least cost in chemicals and flight time.

Whilst watching for markers and assessing the run, sprayers not infrequently collided with trees or one of their greatest enemies: power cables. Strung low across fields, cables can be almost invisible when viewed from the air.

The chemical spillage from the front hopper of G-AMVF is fairly evident in this 1957 photograph. The loads dispensed were often corrosive in nature, and would permeate into every airframe crack and crevice despite the best endeavours of the engineers. G-AMVF survived several British seasons before sale to Australia in August 1960.

When the Tiger Moth evolved from the basic DH60T, the anchorage for the flying wires was repositioned to the root end of the lower mainplane front spars. By moving the entire centre section forward the instructor, who usually occupied the front seat, was permitted unimpeded egress in the case of abandonment.

Having designed an aeroplane that considered parachute escape, it was no great surprise that when Tiger Moths became freely available to the post-war civil clubs, sport parachutists were able to hire them for their lift to height.

The parachutist needed confidence in the pilot who also required a particular awareness; otherwise there were few restrictions. Demonstrating the standard exit technique of the day, with main chute on her back and reserve strapped around her middle, Sue Burges is pictured with a standard Tiger Moth operated by Universal Flying Services from Fairoaks.

As an ardent supporter of the Tiger Club and an integral part of their flying displays, Sue Burges was rewarded in April 1959 with a Tiger Moth specifically converted for parachute dropping and named after her.

The modifications included removal of most of the normal impedimenta from the front cockpit, substitution of the starboard door with a low cut padded decking, and a streamlined windscreen. The walkway on the starboard wing root was widened and a transparent panel let into the trailing edge of the lower mainplane to facilitate sighting over the dropping zone. In all other respects the Tiger Moth, G-APRA, was standard, although surprisingly, faster than all others in the Club at that time.

It may or may not have been as bad as it appears, but the chances are that a few hearts stopped beating at Hewera aerodrome, New Zealand, in March 1986. Cliff Bellingham is attempting to land "on the spot" during the Tiger Club of New Zealand's annual competition. Over correction for a crosswind from the right resulted in a dramatic threepoint arrival which nearly included the starboard lower wingtip. Maximum left aileron and a bootful of left rudder saved ZK-ARJ any lasting embarrassment.

Even though the de Havilland advertisements of January 1932 proclaimed that their Tiger Moth could be equipped with camera apparatus, they could hardly have had this particular configuration in mind.

Whilst the pilot attempts to fly a steady course and speed and height, the passenger, delicately poised on the starboard door ledge, and fully protected from the icy blast, attempts to frame his subject.

The photographer situated in G-ALND must have been incredibly uncomfortable, especially as he was additionally burdened with a parachute. The man with the camera in the formating aircraft might have been equally padded, and whatever the brief, managed to collect in addition to the Tiger Moth, an excellent shot of something looking remarkably like a top secret military installation.

The prototype DH82A, G-ACDA, was registered in March 1933; at the same time, Tiger Moths G-ACDB and G-ACDC were allocated to the de Havilland School, and the trio worked in harmony for seven years until all three were impressed in October 1940. G-ACDA survived the war only to be wrecked in 1979. G-ACDB hit a tree at Sandridge in Hertfordshire whilst on a local flight in June 1941, and was so badly damaged that even DH declined to repair the broken airframe. G-ACDC remained at Hatfield until November 1941 when she was transferred to Stoke-on-Trent and remained there for the duration.

"BB726" was sold back into civilian hands in November 1953, and was restored to flying condition at Croydon in June 1957, repainted as G-ACDC in the house colours of the de Havilland School. Since then, despite several major incidents, G-ACDC has remained the flagship of the Tiger Club, and is recognised as the oldest surviving DH82A. One pre-war DH82 remains airworthy in Sweden and is acknowledged as the world's oldest Tiger Moth.

Family ties in the Tiger Moth fraternity are closer than most, and during the 1962 display season, Flagship G-ACDC was photographed leading the tied-together formation with uprated cousins "The Canon" and "The Archbishop".

This close up shot of the lead aircraft in a tied-together formation was taken from the front seat of a standard Tiger Moth (note the leading edge slat hinge shrouds on the undersurface of the top mainplane) and gives a clear sight of some of the modifications which produced Super Tiger G-APDZ, "The Bishop".

Not seen are the elevators which were increased in area. The lightweight fabric is not exactly evident, but reduced the overall weight by a few pounds.

No matter how impartial the handicapper, or how accurate his assessments, the best and most exciting air races are those in which all aircraft on the start line are of the same type.

Given that each may have a second or two safety pause between wheels rolling, the sight and sound of a circuit stuffed full of racing Tiger Moths is one to be cherished.

Full throttle racing for half an hour was acceptable in the days when engines were cheap and plentiful, but that situation has passed and with it any chance of re-creating a sight such as this when Tiger Moth and Jackaroo aircraft lined up in the National Air Races, and blasted off at full bore when the starter's flag waved each away.

Opposite: July 1961, and Tiger Moth leads Tiger Moth in one of the most critical phases of closed circuit racing. Accurate navigation between pylons, maximum assistance from high or low level winds and a fast aeroplane may not be sufficient to win a race if bad turning costs valuable seconds. Not only is the pylon turn the most crucial, for in anticipation, some pilots have turned inside the line and met with instant disqualification, but it is also the most dangerous when one pilot may not see another. Aircraft have stalled off the turn at low level; have clipped the pylon itself, or just missed it altogether on a murky day. Which way to go then?

The end of a tight race is maybe more exciting than the start, when by keeping low and even lower, split seconds may be gained or lost in the dash for the line; when time stands still and all other competitors gain ground at an astonishing rate.

This head-on shot of a Tiger Moth diving for the finish was taken by a brave photographer. The aeroplane at extreme right is even lower and two more are scraping the contours, dashing for the gap between the trees.

Opposite: Denmark was no storehouse of Tiger Moth parts or expertise during the late Seventies as OY-ECH progressed, although Moths of various types had graced the Danish civil aircraft register for fifty years. So it was perhaps an even greater achievement for an enthusiast like Carsten Ølholm, working in almost total isolation, to present such an immaculate restoration in 1979. This sensational photograph, shot over central Denmark during the late summer of 1986, was produced to illustrate a feature on John Tranum, a pioneer of freefall parachuting. As Carsten Ølholm's Tiger Moth parts company with her most recent passenger, the shades of brown and green camouflage easily merge with the patchwork of fields representing Denmark's agricultural economy, and illustrate the practicability of this military colour scheme when the ultimate intention is *not* to be seen.

In 1960, Air Commodore Christopher Paul, Secretary General of the Air League, sought to renew his seaplane pilot's licence, but discovered to his dismay that the school nearest to his Hampshire home was in Norway. After meetings with interested parties, and the generous funding offered by industry, not to mention a Tiger Moth donated free of charge by Norman Jones of Rollason Aircraft, The Seaplane Club began operations from Lee-on-Solent, an area not unknown to marine aviation of an earlier age.

Later, the Seaplane Club moved base to a freshwater gravel pit near Rye in East Sussex. The aircraft was fitted with a conventional land undercarriage during the winter to allow her to position to and from Redhill for maintenance.

Despite the British weather, the stalwarts of the Seaplane Club operated for over 20 years, gathering a few scars along the way, until on August 27th 1982 the faithful G-AIVW slipped out of a turn, hit the water and was broken into more pieces than even the Tiger Club could restore. But her heart was saved; the trusty Gipsy Major was dried out, overhauled and implanted in a sister Tiger Moth.

With just a touch of drift to counteract the on-shore breezes, Ray Vuillermin kicks in the rudder before wheeling his Tiger Moth VH-GVA, onto the wet sand of an Australian beach. Such a habit might attract swift retribution from the authorities in some countries, but remote, flat, load bearing seashores in Australia and New Zealand offer ideal locations for aerial picnics, conveniently situated at practical flight times beyond access by the masses.

A17-579 was one of the last RAAF Tiger Moths put into store at Tocumwal in 1956, but she was civilianised in 1958 becoming VH-GME. In the early Sixties VH-GME was sold to the Goulburn Valley Aero Club who personalised her as VH-GVA, letters which have been retained ever since through several different ownerships and a major rebuild.

Current one-third owner Ray Vuillermin is pleased to be associated with this particular Tiger Moth, for in 1960 he instructed with her at the McKenzie Flying School under her previous registration, and laid the foundations for a rewarding career as a senior airline captain.

The Cambridge Flying Group is the sole survivor of the untold number of UK clubs and groups that once used Tiger Moth aircraft for initial training. The Royal Newcastle Aero Club at Maitland continues to uphold the Australian tradition.

The reasons are plain enough: Tiger Moths are valuable items of kit and the insurance rates reflect that fact. Current generation pilots mostly are trained on cabin aircraft with heaters and nosewheel landing gear, and the majority have little idea of how to handle a steerable tailskid.

It would appear that yesterday's initial trainer, capable of every aspect of flight, and from which the butcher, the baker and the candlestick maker progressed to Spitfires and jet fighters, is now reserved for whose who show a special ability.

Opposite: The lot of the duster: covered in "super", aircraft and pilot are caught between flights whilst the hopper is replenished. The pilot is Tim Evans-Freke, working at Sheeplands, New Zealand, for the Barr Brothers Company in about 1952.

On average the Ag aircraft were spreading 30 tons per day and in 1950 the record was 55 tons in 9½ flying hours, during which time 220 take-offs and landings had been accomplished.

Altogether 210 Tiger Moths were engaged in agricultural operations in New Zealand, between August 1949 and the last retirement in December 1980.

HMS Eagle completed a major re-fit at Plymouth in 1964 and on June 20th the ship was working-up in the Western Channel, prior to receiving her squadrons.

When it was suggested that Tiger Moths attached to the Britannia Royal Naval College at Dartmouth might care to assist in the ship's training programme, Naval signals establishments were suddenly busy with traffic seeking the necessary approvals.

Four Tiger Moths set off from Roborough in perfect conditions, located and landed on *Eagle,* and struck down prior to the ship altering course out of wind. The landing provided excellent handling practise for the flight deck crew.

No doubt the aviators tested the Wardroom facilities too before leaving, Plymouth bound, after yet another special Tiger Moth occasion.

On the water wishing she could be in the air.

Sea, sun, salt spray, slipstream, and sailing boats; this photograph could have been shot at almost any time between 1933 and 1982, making allowances for the probability that there never was a British Tiger Moth on floats for about thirty of those years.

In fact, the shot was taken after 1967 when the Seaplane Club was based at Lee-on-Solent, and the aircraft operated from slips that had once been the preserve of bigger fish, and were to be again.

To fly a seaplane one has to be a pilot; to taxi and moor one needs a mariner's qualifications and a knowledge of nautical terminologies. The aeroplane is frail like no ship ever was, and a minimal bump on a cloudless day could mean major surgery on the hard, and missed opportunities that might never come again.

Ex-Royal Navy Tiger Moth NL879, one of the quartet which sampled the hospitality offered by *HMS Eagle* in June 1964, joined the Barnstormers Flying Circus as G-AVPJ and was enrolled into a speciality act known as SOW, or "Standing On Wing".

The terminology is slightly inaccurate, as SOW rightly should be SOT, "Standing on Tank", for the lady splicing the mainbrace is strapped to an approved frame attached to centre section pick up points, and is standing on a false floor which spans the tank.

SOW was the invention of Tiger Club stalwart Lewis Benjamin, and following analysis of the problems that were likely to be involved and eventual approval by the airworthiness authorities, it was Benjie himself who made the first live ride on March 4th 1962.

One airshow organiser persuaded the pilot of the SOW aircraft to fly with a stripper, but the plan was cancelled at the last minute on account of the temperature, it was claimed.

7. Towards Immortality

How many people would have guessed that an open cockpit trainer biplane whose prototype first flew in 1931 would, half a century later, become one of the world's most sought after private owner aeroplanes?

Mass production of the Tiger Moth was accelerated during World War Two to finish little short of nine thousand units. The last machine was flown away from the UK's Morris Cowley plant in 1944. Continuous production centred on Europe for 13 years and wartime manufacture and operation in Canada, Australia and New Zealand, coupled with further intense training activity in Africa and India, ensured that not only was the type well represented across the globe, but that it probably was a Tiger Moth in which many an aspiring airman's first serious association with flight began.

The obsolete military trainer was ultimately sold into civil hands at low cost together with masses of inexpensive spares and equipment. Flying instructors and engineers who for years had been in accord with the aeroplane, took little persuading to continue to share their collective and unique experience with a younger, post-war generation, nurtured on aviation.

The Tiger Moth has always been recognised as a superb basic trainer, but she slowly withdrew from that primary role to become a privately owned tourer and aerobatic mount. The aeroplane developed a cult following in Australia, closely

An enthusiast's comment in New Zealand.

shadowed by America after a hundred examples were imported, mostly from Europe. Elsewhere, the phenomenon of Tiger hunting developed more slowly, particularly it would seem in the UK, due possibly to complacency, climatic inspired indifference or the more conservative nature of European vintage aeroplane pilots. For more than half a century, the world has played host to the Tiger Moth. She has seen peace and war and peace again. No task demanded of her has been refused; in return she offered nothing but her protective best. Now she is recognised as a star amongst all aeroplanes; a third generation of pilots enjoys her care in return for personal self-sacrifice, for no ancient aeroplane can be loved without cost.

There is little reason to doubt the Tiger Moth's ability to endure the ravages of time and bureaucratic whimsy and to take aloft pilots of a generation yet unborn. Spares will always be found to maintain her, but whenever the need might come, life-supporting parts must be cast from new jigs. Devotees will accept their burden and bow to their tasks, conscious of the awesome responsibilities bestowed upon them.

Who can guess when the last flight of the last airworthy Tiger Moth might be? Nobody can say; nobody can ever envisage such a situation. Surely, this is the road to immortality!

In honourable retirement, earned after half a life teaching aeronauts to fly, and half tending the land, ZK-AJO is protected by James Aviation of Hamilton.
Between December 1949 and November 1956, this one Tiger Moth, during the course of 6,000 hours flying, spread a staggering 27,900 tons of superphosphate and grass seed. Before retirement, a state which unlike so many others, ZK-AJO enjoys in airworthy condition, she raised her total tonnage to more than 55,000 and is estimated to have earned for her employers more than seventy times her original cost.

The peace and tranquillity of a late summer day in England. A Tiger Moth surveys a hayfield prior to landing, disturbing the larks with the lazy popping of her throttled Gipsy.
The pilot will be glad to get down; to stretch his legs; to retrieve his map from the tailplane strut. de Havilland Field, Crux Easton, Hampshire Downs, 1981. In the 1920s and 1930s, Captain Geoffrey de Havilland lived in a bungalow adjacent to the field and used Gipsy, Hornet and Leopard Moths to commute to and from his office at Stag Lane. His discipline was never to drive if he could possibly fly.

Realising that short-range aircraft could operate nowhere but within the limits of territorial airspace, the New Zealand authorities granted a concession in that the "ZK" national letters need not be displayed. John Crosbie's restoration of "AKC", one of the first batch of all New Zealand built aircraft, is pictured against a rugged landscape at Muzzle Station, on the Clarence River, Marlborough, South Island.

When Sam Cody was flying from Laffans Plain in 1908, he is reported to have tied his aeroplane to a tree to prevent it from being blown away.

In 1982, during the de Havilland Centenary Rally, fifty Moths descended on the Royal Aircraft Establishment at Farnborough on a windy Sunday in July. It was not the weather that caused this Tiger Moth to be restrained by the preserved remains of Cody's Tree, but rather the acute sense of occasion.

Farnborough aerodrome has hosted everything from frail balloons to space vehicles, yet the sight of a famous tarmac occupied by ancient biplanes was recorded with as great an enthusiasm as all the moments of history that ever passed that way.

Late in 1938, Hatfield exported Tiger Moth ZK-AGZ, to New Zealand. Her civilian status was shortlived, for together with more than twenty of her colleagues she was impressed into military service.

Demobilised, the Tiger Moth took up a new set of letters, ZK-ALK, eluding the topdressing companies throughout her working life.

A semi-completed rebuild project, she was bought by John Crosbie of Pukekohe in 1982. ZK-ALK flew again in 1985, resplendent in dark metallic green fuselage and off-white wings, with full span silver letters. The Tiger Moth owners of New Zealand are amongst the world's most enthusiastic, and operate their aeroplanes with a panache generated perhaps by the geographical location of their islands and comparative isolation of properties and airstrips. Onc could easily believe that their's is a different world.

The Canadian Tiger Moth was designed to offer the best possible protection from the vagaries of the North American climate, yet in the hands of enthusiastic civil owners, the DH82C yearned to be like her foreign cousins. Result: off with the lid, on with new decking, doors, windscreens and instrument panels.

In the metamorphosis a few of the original parts tend to get left original! One of the rarely changed items on a DH82C is the steel tube interplane strutting, detected by its narrow chord; the forward rake of the main undercarriage is another vital clue, together with the three piece cowling, an instant improvement on those used elsewhere, but never adapted outside of Canada.

Tiger Moth CF-COV had first worn Royal Canadian Air Force serial number 870 in July 1941 although she served with an RAF EFTS at Bowden, Alberta. Disposed of via the War Assets organisation, she became a civil aeroplane from March 1945, and in 1962 found her way into the care of Bill and Lorraine Orbeck.

Even by American standards, it's some distance between Canada and Hollywood, yet in 1967 the Orbecks and their spotless aeroplane were sharing the tarmac at Burbank with the last of the great piston-powered airliners.

Ten years later, Bill dismantled his beloved Tiger Moth piece by piece, and spent the next seven years and 5,500 hours reassembling her. In company with other vintage biplanes, CF-COV spends once a year on a "scarf and goggles" tour of North America, the crews living under the wings of their aeroplanes; every nut, bolt and fabric stitch a willing sacrifice.

In 1928 Bert Hinkler flew from England to Australia in an Avro Avian covering 11,005 miles in just over 15 days with a total flight time of 128 hours.

For this achievement, Bert Hinkler was elevated to the rank of Honorary Squadron Leader in the Royal Australian Air Force.

Flight Lieutenant David Cyster of the Royal Air Force, late of Lightnings, Phantoms and Gnats, left Dunsfold aerodrome on a foggy morning in February 1978, in his long range Tiger Moth G-ANRF, destination Marseilles. Thirty two days later he landed in Darwin, Australia, having kept the world's press busy with reports of his progress.

David Cyster's tribute to Bert Hinkler was also vindication of his own training and the dependability of his Tiger Moth, 37 years young at the start of the flight. Hinkler's exact route could not be followed due to political changes since the times when aviators drew lines on maps and followed them for days on end.

From the cold of Dunsfold to the sands of Bahrain and a supersonic airliner heading west from Singapore; only the Tiger Moth is timeless.

Not for the first time in history, at Mangalore aerodrome near Sydney, April 13th 1986 saw wings set against wheels.

The quarter mile dash was a competition between Anthony James, representing the Antique Aeroplane Association of Australia, flying his Tiger Moth VH-ALC with eight-year-old daughter Anthea in the front cockpit, and Graeme Lowe of the Historic Racing Car Register of Australia. Graeme was driving a 1936, two litre supercharged, twin OHC Alta, described as "very fast".

Predictably, the Tiger Moth got off to a flying start during her initial climb to racing height of five feet, but Graeme kept his boot pressed hard down and slowly overhauled the aeroplane to win by a short head.

Tiger Moth VH-ALC was one of the hundred British built aircraft supplied to the RAAF under the Empire Air Training Scheme in February 1940, all of which retained their RAF serial numbers until disposal. In 1947 N-9259 was sold to the Association of Australian Auto Clubs, NSW, for a staggering £90.

There are those who cannot bring themselves to think about it; resin re-inforced component parts, not only for use on vintage vehicles, but aeroplanes too.

Feigned animosity from the purists is always greeted with the same rebuff: if the materials had been available *then*, the manufacturers would have used them. They would, of course, but the synthetics hadn't been invented, so the argument forms a circle.

As traditional materials become scarce and expensive, and working skills disappear, vintage aeroplane non-structural parts will inevitably respond to cries for updating in Kevlar and Carbon Fibre. Lightweight, tough, resilient and resistant, hidden under layers of dope and fabric, who would ever know?

Currently building into a high technology Tiger Moth, born of the Eighties and designed for operation until well into the Twenty First century, are these two basic examples of modern material application: a complete set of engine cowlings in Kevlar and rear decking with luggage locker in Carbon Fibre. Non-structural, compounded curves, potentially subject to a high degree of physical abuse: natural points from which to launch the overthrow of beaten aluminium and steamed ply.

Aircraft sold out of the UK Services were often delivered to their new owners with once proud military colours crudely overpainted.

In the mid Sixties, permission was granted for civil aircraft to operate in military markings subject to specified conditions, one of which was the application of standard size civil letters on the fuselage sides and under the wings.

One enterprising owner applied the civil letters to his faultless military scheme in pencil outline which could be identified only by standing close and looking hard, but his initiative was declared unlawful.

By 1975 the authorities had agreed to the carriage of totally authentic service markings, subject only to display of the true registration in the cockpit.

The sight and sound of a number of aeroplanes flying in close formation are senses which cannot fail to thrill even the coldest troglodyte. When the machines are old, Gipsy-powered biplanes, hearts beat faster and eyes moisten as the formation slips into final dressing for its formal salute. After several seasons of anticipation, the de Havilland Moth Club's "Diamond Nine" finally shone from British skies in 1986, booking themselves a permanent encore. Double the necessary nine will always be pooled and practised, on instant call out, ready to maintain the diamond they themselves have fashioned.

Not fierce or flash or even first; the musical progress of nine Tiger Moths in close formation must surely be credited as one of the most emotional displays ever created by this seemingly immortal old friend.

Stars, stripes, chequers, sunbursts, cheat lines, tailwheels, brakes, avionics, red and white and blue. In flight against a deeply shadowed woodland ridge, this Tiger Moth would seem to be a prime candidate for American ownership rather than West German.

D-EEAJ is operated by Michael Dresser and is a widely ranging visitor to European events. Divided by the Atlantic Ocean, geographically if not philosophically, this trim biplane bears a remarkable yet totally co-incidental similarity to the colour scheme of a Californian emigrant.

Previous page: As an initial training aeroplane, the Tiger Moth was endowed with generous abilities in her aerobatic role, and although not classified as one of the world's greatest aerial athletes, in the hands of a good pilot, she could out-perform competitors a quarter her age.

When a professional photographer owns a Tiger Moth, and is a good pilot, then it stands to reason that he will explore all the possibilities afforded by his platform. Torkild Balslev from Denmark was a good pilot, a professional photographer, and owned a Tiger Moth. With the aid of a few simple brackets, some sticky tape and lengths of string, Torkild demonstrates the basic loop.

Hatfield built Tiger Moth No 3956 saw service with the RAF as N-6652 prior to demobilisation and sale to Switzerland in November 1956. By 1969 she was in need of major attention, and was purchased by a small group.

Tiger Moth technical manuals have always been basic, so the group decided that they would detail every nut, bolt, screw, pin and part used during the restoration, and with the aid of archive material supplied by the manufacturer, produce a copiously illustrated, colour-coded manual.

It was an involved and costly exercise, and although the *Tiger Moth Construction Manual* subsequently became a collector's item, the group foundered. What had started with the best intentions finished with heavy financial losses, the sale of the printing plant and ultimately, of the Tiger Moth herself.